How To Unlock Your Creativity

Kathrine L. Holmes

Table Of Contents

How to find Creative juices in the home – how to explore your areas

When it comes to being creative at home, you will want to think about the design of the area. You will want to make sure that it is something that you like and something is like your personality. The creativity of your home will matter when you invite others over. You will want to make sure that the house looks good and not just thrown together. A lot of people are filled with so much energy that they never think about their ideas. You don't want to have too much going on in a room, or your home will look awful. Your home shouldn't like clutter, but it needs to look like it's comfortable and homey. You will want to put a lot of resources together to find the creativity.

When it comes to designing your home, you may want to think about the colors. The colors can be mixed and matched. Something that looks good is when you use neutral colors and then add a bold color to give the room some pop. You will find that your home doesn't have to be the same through out the house. You can get creative with each room; however, they have to move beautifully. Meaning, you have to make the transition between two rooms flow. So if you have a wall way you may want to go lighter in the wall ways and beautiful in the rooms.

When it comes to finding ideas to help you generate some creativity, you may want to look online, in a magazine, or even watch some design shows on the TV. You can find inspiration for your home by going to others. When you visit a friend or family member, you should try to notice some of the things that you liked and some of the things that you didn't like. Then you should try to make it your own and you should try to avoid the things that you dislike. However, don't get take an idea, but build on it. Change it somehow so that you don't seem like a copycat to your friend and also so that you can make it your own.

When you find something that you like, you should try to incorporate it by changing an aspect of it. Do it in a different room, or make the idea out of different material. When it comes to designs you can mix and match colors, but you can also mix and match fabrics. You can do so much with patterns and designs. Your limit is your imagination. You have so many options that you may want to have someone help you make the decisions because you can be overwhelmed with options.

Then once you get some ideas going, you should ask yourself if you think that the idea is you. Does it look like something that you would like? Is it something that you would like to have in your home? There is a difference between something that you like in one person's house and then in yours. Sometimes something that looked nice in someone else's home doesn't look as great in yours because it was apart of the whole package. One little thing doesn't make the room, although it can, it doesn't always. You need to keep in mind that it just might not mesh well with your current décor.

When it comes to decorating your home, you may never know what you like until you place it in your home or try it in your home, and then it just might not look well. Don't get frustrated because paint can be repainted, fabrics can be returned, and everything can work out.

Without having goals you can never succeed

When it comes to setting goals, you will notice that it will help you choose a path for your life and to help keep your life pushing forward. You will know what you want to achieve and where you place your concentration. You will be able to spot all the things that will sidetrack you or distract you from the main goal. When you have a goal and plan, you will find that you will know when you are on tract with the goal and when you are not. When you set your goals properly, you will find it to be motivating and help you stick with the main focus. Every time you reach a goal, you will find yourself wanting to keep moving forward. You want to be able to reach for something and be truly focused on it or you'll never reach anything. Goals help you stay on the right path and they help you stay out of trouble.

You will find that your mind is a wonderful tool and your life will be designed to reach for your dreams and live your life the way that you have designed your life. You are able to focus on what you want for your life and then when you set a clear and comprehensive goal you know that you can have such an achievement. Your achievements are marked because you worked so hard for them. When you place a goal on paper, you are able to mark a path for where you want your life to go. Then you are able to physically see that you can do whatever you need to or achieve your goal.

Who uses goals? Well, everyone uses goals to help them make it to their dreams. Businessmen and women, athletes, students and more use goals to help them make it to their dreams. Without goals, you must not have dreams because you cannot reach your dreams unless you set your goals down and a game plan. When you set goals, you are able to motivate yourself and be able to visualize who you are. You may find that you may have to do a lot of research for you to be able to set your goals properly. You are also going to have to organize your time and find some resources to help you make the most out of your life.

For you to properly set a goal, you must be specific. You need to think about all the details of your goal and what you have to do to meet your goal. You want to make sure that you have everything covered in the plan. When you aim for a goal, you will find things that will distract you. Have a plan when it comes to the distractions. Do you have a friend to help keep you on track? Do you have anyone who cares enough to help you find the path that you stray away from? Hopefully you can find a backup plan to your problems.

Why are goals so important? Goals give a person direction, and if you don't have direction then you have no other option by to wonder. Wondering is okay when you are very young, but when it comes to being a responsible adult you are pressured by society to have goals and plan. You are expected to know what you want out of life and how to get to your life goal at a very young age. When you are twenty or three you will find yourself wondering what you want for your life. If you set a goal early, you can at least have some direction in life, but as you grow you can always change your goals to something that you want.

How to Bring nature into your life

Do you ever have the time to reduce your stress and relax? Well you can by brining nature into your life. You will find that you will feel better about yourself and life when you allow nature into your life. Many people believe that your environment influences the way that you feel.

First, you should go out and take a walk. When you are taking a walk, you will find that nature will give you a lot of visual pleasure. You will benefit from the exercise and you can have time to think and get away from everything. You can soak up some sunlight and vitamins from the sun and breathe some healthy, fresh air. You will also notice all the beautiful things that is in nature. Even if you just take a walk, around the block, you will find some inspiration and you will find that your stress is also relieved a bit. If you can have a lot of good downtime when you go to a nearby park, you can sit on a bench and watch the world pass you by. What you see, what do you feel, all the answers to life's problems can be found by sitting on a park

bench. You can watch the world go by without even once stopping to give you notice. You can take in all the serenity and in the silent air; you will find the answers to what you are looking for. Nature does not just allow you to relax from the daily grind, but it also helps you with all your problems. T
Nature is inspiring.

If you don't need answers, but something to help you relax and comfort you, you may want to plant a garden. When you plant a garden, you will find that you are needed and you can focus on something that seems so basic. You don't have to worry about the plants other than water and feeding it. You can pull grass and weeds out of your frustration. Garden helps relieve some anger and frustration. You don't have to have a big garden, just something to care for in your spare time. Something to keep your mind off from focusing on the negative things in life; landscaping can be very peaceful too. It will help your home look welcoming and it will allow you to get all your feelings out and pour all your emotion into something that needs it.

If planting doesn't work, you should take a chair and place it in front of a window. Open the blinds and sit in the sun with your eyes closed. Feel the warmth that nature has. Feel the comfort of the light touching your shoulders. You will become inspired and you will feel free for a few moments.

When you do this, you may be able to find your inner peace. You should allow nature into your home to help to help you feel comforted and relaxed. You should bring in rocks, feathers, and a flower, anything that you can find in nature. This way you can always find comfort in nature. A great thing to have in your office is a water fountain. This way you can always have the calming sounds of nature.

Even if you place a bowl of fruit on your kitchen table, you will find that it will be appealing to the eye and give the room some positive energy. Nature will help you get through the day and will help you to be inspired so that you can continuously be creative and inspired. Nature is the best way to relax.

How to feel more creative in life

You know what people lack the most any more. It is not money, nor materialistic items. It is creativity. Some people will find that they have so much creativity that they can't hold themselves back from ideas, but others seem to struggle with creative ideas. There are plenty of ways that you can get more creative; you just have to get more creative. That is in activities. You need to make sure that you are doing plenty of activities that stimulate the mind. For starters, how about trying to do a puzzle of some sort? The best are the crossword puzzles. Crossword puzzles stimulate creativity because most of the time you will not have any clue to what the answer is, but you can try to come up with suitable ones to see how far you can get until nothing matches anymore. When you do a lot of mind activities, you will find that you will be able to think much clearer. The brain will be use to the stimulation and soon the creativeness will pour right out of you.

If you're not into mind games, how about a jog? Have you ever noticed that your best ideas come from when you work out? When you work out you are able to let go of all your stress and your mind becomes clear. You can think and soon all these creative ideas will start developing and then more. If you exercise on a daily basis, you will find that your mind is enhanced, your attitude is enhanced, and so is your creativity. You'll feel free and be able to do your job better when you exercise. If this is not your type of stimulation, try a book!

When you read, your mind becomes a world of wonder. You can think and imagine things that you never thought about before. You will find that a good book will help you get out of your character and into another. You'll be able to think like a comedian, a romantic person, or even a dramatic person. You can find a lot of inspiration in a good book. If you need to get creative you should read something to help influence you, or you can also watch TV.

The TV is a box of information and ideas. All you have to do is allow yourself to be influenced. Watch some day time TV and see what is on. Watch the commercials for some humor. Whatever it is that you are looking for can be found right there in the TV.

If you get better ideas from resting, you should go take a nap. When you take a nap, you allow yourself to drift into a wonderland that only you can control. You can feel free to comes up with ideas and be inspired by a dream because there is no one there to judge your ideas. All you have to do is relax and stretch your muscles. Lay down with a clear mind for an hour and you're sure to wake up with a mindful of ideas.

Being creative is not hard when you have something or someone to inspire you. Think about all the things in life that you like and all that your hate. Sit and watch strangers pass you by on the street and try to guess where they came from and where they are going. You will be able to get more creative when you take the time to be creative.

They key to creativity is to let your creativity flow freely or you will never find anything that will inspire you.

How to open your inner feelings

It's hard to be open with others. You never know what will come from your vulnerability. You may find that you would like to be open to your inner feelings, but you are afraid of how others will perceive you. If you really would like to open your inner feelings up to yourself and to others, you need to let go of all your perceived notions. You have to allow yourself to be who you are by not allowing others to hurt you. You may tell yourself that you want to go for something and you don't care what the other one thinks, but if you really didn't care, you wouldn't have to give yourself a pep talk.

It's hard to open your inner feelings up to others, but how can you overcome all your troubles? Well if you really want to open your inner feelings up to another, you must care for this person greatly. They must also care about you a great deal. If you find it hard to let your feelings out in the open, then you may want to ease into the situation. You don' want to tell someone you love them without going out with them. You need to think small and work your way up. When you take the time to express yourself, you will find that when the time comes to open up, you feel more comfortable in doing so. You should know that you are going to sometimes want to spill more than needed, but be patient and allow the moments come to you. Mystery is one aspect of love. You must always have the mystery. Keep the person on the edge of their seat by beating around the bush. If you would feel more comfortable stating your emotions in an indirect way, then go for it.

However, if you still feel uncomfortable to spill your emotions when the time comes, you can always talk to your partner about how you feel about talking to them about the serious feelings that you have. This way you can get them to understand that this is a very difficult process for you. Another thing, be honest. Be honest to the other person and to yourself. Make sure that you aren't trying to talk yourself out of another feeling just because it is looked down upon by society. You are how you are and that can never change. The only thing that will change is rather or not that you are being true to yourself. Sometimes it's very hard to do so, but it's so important.

If you want to open up to yourself, you may want to start things off by setting your priorities. You need to list what you really care about and what you don't. Then at the end of the list make sure that you are keeping in check. If you find that you feel one way by do things another, then you aren't being honest to yourself and you have to be brave to do so.

If you need to learn how to open up to others, you may want to think about waiting for the moment to strike. You will know when that moment is deep in your heart. Just listen to your instincts and follow through with all the plans, emotions, and ideas so that you can act on your instincts. You may also want to go through the buddy system for support. The buddy system is when you lean on some one for moral support and they try to encourage you to reach for your goals. Your best friend can be the best supporter that you may ever find.

How to open your feelings to others

Opening your feelings up to others can be tricky. You may not know who to trust, and if you want to trust them. When it comes to expressing your feelings to a possible love, it is even harder. No one likes being rejected, but if you truly care for the person, you would want to tell him or her and hope for the best response. For those who have been seeing someone for some time now and know that they care deeply for someone you may want to think about the following.

First, when it comes to opening up your feelings to others you need to try to incorporate some romance, creativity, and being unique. This means that you shouldn't quote s a line from some recent movie that you have watched. You need to think about the words that you would like to use to help express or define your feelings to them. It's all about timing and the right words; however, if they care about you too, then you shouldn't feel pressured. However, if you care about some one there is always pressure because of fear. The best way to show someone that you care is through your words and then followed by your actions.

When it comes to expressing your feelings about someone, you should first think bout why you feel so strongly about them. You may want to place your feelings into a poem. You don't have to read them the poem, but you will discover your true feelings through a poem. You need to allow yourself to be inspirited by the warmth and happiness that you feel when you are around this person and how much you need them in your life. The poem will help you choose your words as well. Once you have the words down, you need to think about the romance.

When it comes to romance, you may want to think about when you are going to announce feelings and how. Wait until the moment comes to you. Maybe you will want to go back to the place where you first met or kissed. You can do whatever you want to show the person that you care about them or that you love them. Try to get creative with your feelings and ideas. You should never stress about it, because it is more than likely that they feel the same about you.

When you say, "I love you" you need to mean it. How do you show that you mean it? You show meaning threw your actions. Make sure that your actions say the something that you express with your words. Make sure that you don't tell them that you love them and then ignore them for the rest of the day. You need to tell that special someone that you are in love, then cuddle with them, and make them feel safe, secure, and that you are honestly being sincere. You will want to make sure that you mimic your words with your actions.

However, actions speak louder than words. If you show the person how much they mean to you, you may not have to say I love you verbally. Your actions can say it all. Make sure that you are supportive, comforting, and encouraging. When you show the other person that you are supportive, comforting, and encouraging, you are telling them that you love them. To allow yourself to open up to someone, you may want to think about making a list of what you feel for them, why you feel for them, and reasons why you should trust them with your heart. This will make you feel much more secure when it comes to verbally expressing yourself.

How to Learn to be more communicative

Communication is the basis of our relationships with friends, co-workers, and even lowers. It's is a wonderful thing when you are on the same page, but sometimes the miscommunication can cause you to have problems with those who matter the most to you. You need to make sure that you listen and state your feelings, opinions, ideas, and so on effectively.

First thing first, you need to practice listening. Listening does not count that you notice every other word and say "uh huh", but you have to learn how to focus on the speaker and what the message is. You need to really practice this to get good at. You should set aside at least ten minutes or so every day to catch up on life. You need to communicate and listen to others about their day. When you get home from work, you should ask your roommate, lover, or family how their day was. Then you need to stand in front of then with eye contact and take in every word that they say. You should never ask and then walk away, it's rude and the miscommunication or lack of communication can be a serious strain on friendships and relationships.

When it comes to listening, you need to know the difference between listing and hearing. Hearing is the act and process that your body goes through for you to get a message from another's voice. However, listening is when you focus on the person and what they are saying with full comprehension of what the conversation is about. You should make sure that you are able to focus on the person, before you take the time out to start a conversation.

Next, you need to be able to respond to the person and the conversation. You should never ramble but just get to the point. You will need to talk while in turn and not over others. If you are excited, your excitement will become passion when you wait your turn to speak. In addition, you need to make sure that you choice your words carefully. Say, what you mean, and mean what you say. Don't allow your emotions to blind you. You should never say anything out of anger. Never allow your emotions to distract you from effectively communicating with someone. You should also be aware that both men and women talk differently. Women need to talk to you for emotional reasons and men like to report. Men like to get to the point and then carry on about something else. They tend to be one with the most communication ADD. Basically, if you are taking to a different sex, you need to consider the way they like to communicate, you may need to be straight to the point, and you may need to take their emotions inconsideration.

Also, to be good at communicating, you need to know how to read people's body language. You should take inconsideration of their posture, tone, and facial expressions. They may be saying one thing, but their body is saying another thing. That is why you need to be careful about your own verbal and nonverbal communication. You need to make sure that they are both conveying the same message or the other person may get a little confused. Also, if you don't pay attention to your messages, then you might even offend or send the wrong message. When it comes to communication, you need to think about your environment too. Is it too noisy, should you go somewhere quite? You want to make sure that your environment cannot distract you or those who you want to communicate with or you might find that they do not get the same message that you are trying to convey.

How to open your life to be with others

When it comes to opening your life up to others, you may feel a little hesitant. You may not want to open yourself up because you are uncomfortable with new people or you have mistrusted people in the past, but you need to find ways to overcome the issues and to allow yourself to open your heart to others. You will find that sustaining and maintain friendships and relationships can be very hard, but they are also interesting and can be passionate. You never know what a relationship or friendship might bring you in the future, but one thing is for sure, you need to learn how to get over the past and live for the future.

When it comes to new relationships there are some problems that will show up early and some that will show up later in the relationship. You need to realize that the ups and downs are a part of every friendship and can be a vital part of the relationship. You need to know that they are truly in the relationship or friendship and if they are ready to give up one the first bump comes up, and then you may need to find a new person to have a relationship or friendship with.

When it first comes to opening yourself up, you will want to take things slowly. Make sure that you build a strong foundation before you start having strong feelings. To first open up, you will need to put yourself out there and find someone who you would like to get to know. Once you have found someone, you should begin with all the small talk and slowly work the relationship up to a status that you are happy with. It's always best to start any relationship off with a friendship; because you will find that your relationship with them will be solid and worth, all the effort that you later will put into the relationship to sustain it. Sometimes you will find that you will need to be the one who leads the relationship and sometimes when you need to follow. This is just the daily give and take of any relationship.

Another good way to start opening up is to let things lie where they are for a while. You don't need to focus on a new relationship, you need to surround yourself with those who you love and cherish. You need to give and take for the relationship, but you should also have a strong identity outside of the relationship so that you can be secure in the relationship.

Once you have built a strong friendship, you can then turn it into a strong and solid relationship. Again, taking it day-by-day and step-by-step. If you don't rush a relationship, you will find that you will be placing trust and commitment to a person worth the trouble. If you go slowly, you know that they are someone who you will comfortable opening up to. You should never open up to anyone who makes you feel uncomfortable because it will add stress and concern to your list of issues.

You will know how and when you can open up to the ones that are close to you. You will feel a bond between you two that is strong and secure. You will feel secure in the relationship because of the understanding that you have in the relationship or friendship, which is very important to anyone who wants to open his or her feelings and heart.

Security is necessary if you plan to be open and close to, someone and it can be built by having an honest relationship or friendship.

How to realize there is a purpose to life

Have you ever wondered what you purpose in life is? Well, you should know that your purpose in life has nothing to do with your job. It has nothing to do with all the things on your to do list. It has nothing to do with your goals. Your purpose in live is all about what you were put on earth and why you exist. Perhaps, this sounds too deep for some, but it doesn't have anything to do with religion either. It has to do with defining yourself and how you are. Maybe your purpose on life was to help save he world and maybe your purpose in life was to share your happiness and optimistic personality with everyone that you meet. Your purpose is in life is not like anyone else. Everyone has a purpose in life that is unique.

So how to you find your purpose in life? This is a question that everyone needs to ask himself or herself. Their purpose lies within them. All you have to do is learn how to empty your mind of all your perceived notions about yourself. You need to believe that there is a purpose and that it has nothing to with anything materialistic. First, you should know that it takes time to learn how to relax and let go. You may need to sit in a room for twenty minutes every night before you are able to let go of what happened that day and focus on nothing.

Here's a tip to help you find your purpose in life. Take out a piece of paper and what the phrase, "What is my intended purpose in life?" Then right the first answer that comes to mind without thinking. Then repeat and try to come up with a new answer each time. You will know what answer is the true purpose when you read it and it overwhelms you with emotion. I may take you twenty minutes to an hour to find out your purpose, but you will find your purpose in life regardless. The first couple times you will notice that your answers are closed, but as you go on with the activity, you will find that the answers are truer to the heart. At one point, you will find yourself resisting the activity. You will want to do something else, but it is because you fear the truth. Everyone fears the truth. When you notice some resistance, you will find your true purpose in life within minutes. When you do this, you need to be alone and with no distractions. This means you cannot do this in front of the TV. If you truly feel you do not have a purpose in live then you should start from there and see what your answers turn into.

Your purpose may be so simple, but the best purpose in the world. Your purpose may end up being to live, love, and laugh as much as possible, or it could be to energize the world with great ambitions and peace. Your purpose will also reflect your personality. If you are a peaceful person, then you may find that your purpose in life is to balance out some of the craziness of the world.

When you begin this activity, you may know what your purpose is in life, but it could be the complete opposite in the end. Why? Because sometimes we lead our lives in hopes to be approved by others like friends, family, and close loved ones. You may get lost in other people's dreams, but once you do this activity, you will find that everything will work out for you in the end.

How to realize you can be more in life

When it comes to realizing what you can do with your life, you have to have goals and some ambition. You need to figure out what you need to do in life and what you want to accomplish before it's over. You need to find the simply joys of life and you should surround yourself with family and friends who love you. To realize what you can be in life, you need to know how to set some goals and find yourself. Once you have set some goals and found your purpose in life, you will be eager to wake up in the mornings and you will also realize all that life is willing to offer you.

When it comes to setting goals for yourself in your life, you need to first find out who you are, and what type of person you are, and where you wish to go. When it comes to finding out who you are, you need to list three words the describe you. Then give the words meaning, by giving examples. You then you need to think about where you are in life and where you would like to be. Once you figured out where you would like to be, you have just set a goal for yourself.

When it comes to goals, you need to make sure that you have set a goal that is possible for you to reach. Then you should make sure that your goals are something that you really would like to pursue and not something that sounds nice aloud or on paper. Once you have verified what the goal is and that it is feasible, you need to compare it to your ethical and moral standards. Is it something that you would lookdown on others for, or is it something that you truly would like to seek and is consistent with your morals?

If you are setting your life goal, you will also have to set some milestones in your goal to make sure that you are progressing towards a goal. You will want to make sub goals for all the areas of your life. You will need a goal for your personal life, spiritual life, social life, financial/work like, physical well being, and your mental well being. Once you have hit the tiny goals, you will know that you are moving forwards towards your purpose and goal in life. Make sure that you jot the goals down in a positive way so that you are eager to pursue them. If you ever find yourself bitter about a goal or negative about a goal, then you should forget the goal and write a new one, because it has to be something that you truly want in life.

Once you have all the sub goals in mind, you should think about writing your entire goal in detail like a life plan. When you have a life plan, you will have something to reach for and to work hard towards. You will find that there is more motivation and successful for people who write a life plan.

Then once you have your life planned out, you should look over and review your goals. Make sure that your goals are feasible, but challenging. Once you have reviewed the plan, it is time to take action. You need to find ways to seek the plan's goals out and to find the success that you hope for. You need to come back to your plan every now and then for some motivation. When you get off track, you can easily come back by reviewing everything that you wish to achieve in this lifetime.

How to realize your energy comes from within

When it comes to your inner energy, you will find that you have all the strength within you to get up and achieve or seek out whatever it is that makes you happy. You should try to seek out a happy, healthy, and fulfilling life. When your time is up, you will want to be able to say that you've done it all, however, many people fear the end because of all that there is that they want to seek. What is it that you wish to seek out? You need to be able to define what you want so that you can dig up all the energy inside yourself to help you achieve your goals. You should also try to realize what type of energy that you have and how to tap the energy out of you when you are trying to seek a goal.

First, would you say that you are normally an optimistic or pessimistic person when it comes to your overall attitude of your life? If you find yourself positive, then you should consider yourself fortunate to not let others drag you down. If you are negative then you need to find ways to turn your negative into a positive. One way to convert your energy is to seek a message therapist. That's right a message therapist, especially one that specializes in Reikki message. This is a type of message that allows all your negative energy out and to fill you with hope, peace, and love. Not to mention it will help you with your goals in life. You will find that when your energy was been cleansed, then you will be able to carry on with your life with all intentions of reaching for the stars. When you have positive energy you will find the strength to do anything, now all you have to do is use it.

How are you able to tap into your energy to help you deal with some of your goals and the obstacles that you need to pass? Well, the only way for you to use it is to realize that you have the power to do whatever you want, and that you allow yourself to seek your goals. For you to get the energy to meet a life-changing goal, you need to know that you are capable of doing it and you have to have passion. It is the passion that will make your goals obtainable. You need to want it so bad that you got to do it and if you want something that bad, there is nothing that will ever stop you from getting it. All you have to do is know what you want out of life. If you can define what it is that you want then you will be able to seek all that you have set in mind.

Once you can define the goals and who you are, the picture will come in much clearer. You will notice that your goals will seem to become closer and you will be able to work your way up to some of the life goals that you have met. When you hit a rough spot you have two options; either push forward or quit. Do you really want to quite, or do you want to see it through? If you have passion, your decision will be automatic. You will find a way to meet your goals and to have everything that you ever dreamed of come true. However, it is hard and you need to put a lot of effort forth. If it is something that you truly want then you will find a way to achieve it.

How to Be in touch with life helps you be creative

When it comes to being creative, you can find all the ways to make up for what you lack. If you could get more in touch with life than you would find that your creative side will grow and you can embrace it. If you take the time for yourself and live for the moment, your life will be more than satisfying. The great thing about life is that you can't predict it, if you could get in touch with your creative side by finding how to life right, you will be much happy. So how does a person live right? If you eat and exercise on a daily basis, you will be able to stay healthy. If you stop planning every minute of your day, you will be able to live. Really live is the point to all existence. People go through life without ever stopping to enjoy it. If you can stop every now and then and enjoy your life you will be happier and more productive at your work.

What you should do, what everyone should do, is take a weekday off and do nothing. Stay home and do the laundry or go to the mall for some time for yourself. You should take the day off and do whatever it is that you need to do. You need to make sure that you take care of yourself every now and then. It's okay to call off work or place one day aside for just you. Make sure that the kids are at school and that your mate is off to work. All you need is one day of hassle free time. When you take the time, you should not think about yourself as a mother or a wife, a student, or anything. You should just care about yourself for one day.

That is one way of getting in touch with life. Anther way is to keep yourself in the scene. You should expose yourself to new and interesting things. Every weekend you should do something that is unique. You can go to the ballot, an art show, a concert, anything that is creative. When you go you need to be open minded about it, allow yourself to be inspired. If you can, try to take it all in, and then put a journal together and make sure that you write down everything that you felt at that moment. Then in a day or two review your thoughts and the inspiration from the journal will make your creativity flow. You have no idea how much you are affected every day by the media and the things that you see. Everything that we watch, listen to effects creativity. Allow yourself to be inspirited by the art or the performance.

If you don't like to go out, you can always watch the shows in the comfort of your own home. If you flick through the channels, you can hear and see all the heroes of the world and their ideas and creations. There is so much you can discover or think that you never would because the information was presented to you. The TV is a link to other worlds and ideas and thoughts, creations. Watching TV a few hours a night will get your creativity flows going and you will find that your be more knowledgeable about the world and be creative in designs and other things.

If you took the time to look around, you'll be able to find the world. You can see the world in the comfort of your own home and you can experience the world by trying out new things. If you could give it a shot, you will be pleased with the results.

How to live life to be creative

Do you think your life is boring? Well, you never know what kind of fun you may find is you get out and enjoy some of the things that are going around you. You need to go from your old routine to no routine. When you have a daily routine, your life is going to seem like it drags on and on. You need to mix it up a little.

One way to mix it up a little is to take another way to work or your destination. It may be longer, but it'll be a change and by the time you get to work, you will be ready and willing to handle anything that you are given. You can do a lot of little things to change your day. You can take one way to work and then another way home, just so you don't get in a routine in the morning either. Like eat breakfast and then get dressed; do anything to get out of your routine.

Then when you can you should go out and try new things. Go to a new restaurant and order something that you've never had. When you try new things, you'll seek out interesting things. You may want to go and do things that you normally wouldn't do. Like go to the ballet or the art show. There's always a craft show to go to. Anything that would make your day extraordinary will do. Once you have begun to seek things out that are new and interesting, you will want to keep it up, because the experience will make your life more exciting.

Now some people say that if you want an exciting life, you should hit the clubs, however, you should only go for the conversation and dancing. You don't need to drink to have an exciting life. Speaking of dancing, have you ever thought about taking a dance class? You can take classes for club dancing, ballroom dancing, tango, rumba, and more. You usually don't have to have a partner either.

There is a lot of things that you can do to improve your life and these are just a few suggestions. You can do anything that you would like to seek out as long as it is not part of any routine. With routines, they are great because they keep us on time, however, they also can be depressing. When you feel that your life is one day played over and over again, that's when you need to either drop the routine or change it. You can think about all the little things that you can change the night before and then wake up and make a change. When you change your routine every now and then, your spirits will lift up.

Also, it may not be your routine, but the people in your routine. You may just need to get out there and meet some more people. That's doesn't mean you should be pressured to find a boyfriend or girlfriend, even finding some new crowds at work or at the clubs would be find. As long as you're happy that's all that matters. The point of change is to get closer to leading a happy and fulfilling life. Whatever it takes, you should try to get closer to that goal. Everyone wants to be happy, but it can take awhile to be happy. It can take awhile to figure out what exactly it is that makes your happy. Have fun while trying to fill the void by seeking new things and new people and get creative with your life routine.

How to process to inner peace

When it comes to finding inner peace, it's hard. So many things make a person feel uncomfortable with their body and mind. There is always that one person who feels the need to bring everyone down. You need to find inner strength to not care, however, no matter how much we say we do not care, we always do. So how to do you find inner peace?

Here is one thing you can do; you can do a self-id activity. First, grab a pen and paper and make two columns. In one column, you will want to write everything that you like about yourself, and then everything that you want to work on yourself. Usually, when it comes to the things that you like it's about personality and the things you hate is your appearance. You should try to mix up the things that you like and dislike so that you don't get one type of aspect. We are harder on our physical looks because that's what others see. They judge because of their own insecurity, so you should never take any comment about yourself to heart.

Now that you have your list, pick three things that you dislike that you wish you could change. Then you can work out a plan to change things. You don't have to change things dramatically. Like if you dislike your weight, take a walk. If you take a walk everyday, you'll find that you'll feel a bit better about yourself.

The second part of finding inner peace is excepting who you are. There is nothing wrong with anything about your body or personality. Basically, you are who you are. There are things that you are going to be able to change, and there are going to be things that you can't. You'll know the difference because if you want to change something you can. Your imbibitions will help you fix everything that you want to. You need to take in consideration of your physical needs and your mental needs. If you can take care of your needs, then you will find acceptance, as well as, inner peace.

The only way that you can sustain your inner peace is not listen to other's talk. People love to talk other's down. They do this because of their own insecurities and you have to accept that. There is going to be someone that notices everything wrong with your outfit or house and so on. You need to be able to let the comments roll off your back. Don't carry that negative weight around or your energy will be off balance.

Also to sustain your inner peace, you have to take care of yourself. You need to watch out for yourself so that you don't feel dependent on anyone. Once you find that you are dependent on someone, this is when you allow them to emotional hurt you. It's a sad thing, but true. When it comes to taking care of yourself, you have to set goals for yourself and meet them, and if you miss your goal, then you need to focus on all the hard work that you did and be proud of yourself. There are a lot of goals that you will miss and lot that you hit. You should always be proud of yourself because of all the hard work that you have done. Finally, the last tip to help you sustain inner peace has to do with Maslow's hierarchy of needs. You need to take care of your basic survival needs, then your safety needs, followed by your social needs, then with ego needs, and then self actualization. To find true peace you need to be happy with who are you and where you are. It may take a lifetime to get there, but it is worth it.

How to expressing yourself

Sometimes when you are in a small group or even with friends or family, you may find a hard time expressing yourself. It's because of your insecurities that you hard back. Basically, everyone is afraid of getting made fun of or being put down. People don't handle rejection very good so they try to avoid rejection and acceptance. This is not the way that you should go about your life. People find change throughout their life. Don't resist it. If you take the time to get to know your new co-workers, you will find that they are worried about the same things that you are.

One way to feel comfortable about expressing your views is to learn about the points that others make and why you feel the way, you do. This is great when you go to college to master something. With education comes security; you can talk to others at work because you have a common bond with each other. You know how to do the job so you should be proud enough to tell others. If you can express your educational views, you may find that the small group may use your suggestion or they may build on it, but it is still part of the solution. Even if it doesn't seem like they like your suggestion, you have just inspired them to come up with something big. You're still part of the final solution.

Also, when it comes to work, you should feel comfortable around your co-workers for the fact that you have spent a lot of time with them. You have gotten to know them and know their opinions. If you think that you are going to clash with your co-workers, all you need to do is state "this is just my opinion" and then express yourself. That way the group doesn't feel like your being overbearing. When you are sensitive to the needs of the group, the group will be more likely to hear you out.

Another thing is that you need to realize that there are a lot of people who love and care about you. There are going to be times that you will conflict with them, but there are other times when things just seem to work its way out. However, if you don't express yourself, then you will never be able to be yourself in a relationship and friendship. If you can't be yourself in an relationship, then you might as well not even be in one because it's pointless. If you can't show them the real you, then they will come to expect things out of your personality and you will find yourself lost.

Once you get to know people you'll feel comfortable around them, but it's hard getting to know people. You can feel like you need to watch this, that, and you cannot be yourself holding back. So, what should you do to get to know people? Well, you should think about it this way: if they are new in your life you should introduce yourself and show the real you, because if they don't like it, they don't have to.

You can't be friends with everyone, nor should you try. It's good to have people who don't like you as much because they are the ones that will be critical of you. They make you reach for better ideas and goals. So if anyone ever criticizes you, take it, because you will be able to defend your ideas with education, as well as, critique your ideas to be better. Criticism helps you look at your ideas and make them stronger, so don't be afraid of it.

How to understand your possibilities are limitless

What comes from limiting yourself? Not much. When you limit yourself on ideas and thought, you can't come with a good, logical solution. The best actions came from a terrible idea. So if you think for a moment that your ideas are horrible, give them a second thought. There are so many ways that a wacky idea has helped businesses in America and people in general to make great decisions. Even when you come up with the wacky ideas, you are still being productive. The off the wall chances usually end up inspiring others to seek better ideas. They inspire you to come up with things that do work. You know the difference between being a leader and a follower? The difference is that a leader has no limitations. There are so many people who limit what they can do and limit their ideas so that they sound stupid and be judged, but if everyone limits themselves, who is going to come up with the good solutions? If you were in a group with others who limit themselves, then your group would be worthless if you limit yourself.

So what if you do let yourself go, what does it mean to be limitless? To understand your possibilities you have to think about the universe. Earth is just one piece of the universe. You are just one piece of earth. The universe has no end. You have so much room that you cannot even understand it. When you do not limit yourself, you are up for anything. You will know how to react and quickly. People who do not hold themselves back are the ones that end up being heroes because they did not hesitate. You may find that by not limiting yourself you can save a life, save a business, save yourself. You can do so much more than anyone. You can see things in ways that others cannot. You will be able to see the big picture and the small picture. You have the opportunity to see everything.

The great thing about not limiting yourself is that you have more of a possibility to go places. You will be able to find love, friendships, career opportunities, and you will be able to achieve all your goals. You should be able to find everything that you seek by being open to the world. The possibilities of what you will accomplish and what you will see will be huge because you open yourself up to the world and those around you. When it comes to being a manager, they try to math others conform, however, if you are a leader, you will be open to your employees, and you will have one of the most successful stores or departs because you do not limit your resources of ideas.

A leader needs to be able to think on all levels. You have to be able to focus on the small task and then how it will affect the over all task. To do that you have to find a lot of resources to help you (like listening to your employees) and be open to your own ideas Remember, that no idea is a bad idea, it's just not complete. Bad ideas are what helps a person to grow and find the best solution. Bad ideas are the basis for great ideas. If you were to limit yourself you would never be able to find the best idea.

The difference between someone stuck in a job and someone who is in a job is the fact that they are open to new things and ideas. They look at things with a positive and not a negative. Don't be stuck at a job, allow yourself to make the best out of it.

You can't succeed without pushing yourself

Have you ever heard of the old saying "You can do anything that you want if you put your mind to it"? Well, it's true. All you have to do is want something so bad that you'll never stop until you reach your goal. Here are some ideas to help you push yourself to reach your goals.

First, when you make goal, you do it, so that you can meet them. You need to know just how much work you have to do to meet a goal. You have to focus on your goals constantly. You have to make sure that everything that you do will bring you closer to your goals and not push you a step back. That may have to do with your finances and other things like your attitude. You have to look at your goal and make milestones so that you know that you have made some progress. Each time that you hit your milestone you can feel good knowing that you are pushing yourself forward.

You should also limit your ambitions. Even though you should never limit your possibilities, id you limit your ambitions you will find that you can focus on one task at a time. You may have to reach duel goals, but anything more than two at a time, will confuse you and screw everything up. Remember, baby steps are how you get to where you want in life. You need to focus on one or two goals at a time, but make sure that the one won't hinder the other. Once you have decided that you have picked a goal that you really need to achieve first, you can then move on to focusing on the goal, and then go back to the others so that you can reach all your goals.

Before you start all the hard work, you may want to make sure that your goal is what you really want. Don't be general in listing your goals. You have to be specific. You need to give yourself deadlines and a plan on how to get to your goal before the deadline. Once you have the plan, you will find that your hard work will be organized and it will pay off in the end. You should also plan for the end result what you will do when all the hard work as paid off.

If you have a goal and somehow to celebrate you will be more likely to actually work hard when you have a plan.

When it comes to the hard work, you will find that you will need to take things one step at a time. You can't skip some of the steps in your plan and expect it to work out exactly how you planed it. You got to follow the plan and stay on task with the plan. If you stray from the path, then you can bring yourself back in and try to make up for the time that you missed by working harder, however, if you do your best to stick to the plan, you shouldn't have to go the extra mile. A well thought out plan will save you time and money. It will help you to achieve your goal quickly, however, you need to find a way to stay with the goal, and it can be hurtful. You may find that the steps are harder to stick with than to do. This is when the hard work really gets hard. If you really want to reach your goals, you are going to need to be disciplined and focused.

How to find peace within yourself

It's hard finding inner peace when you have a million things on your to do list. You may find that your inner peace seems far-fetched, but there are ways that you can find your inner peace and divine happiness. You need to find ways to let go of your tiresome life and learn how to deal with the struggles and stress that you may find through your day. What you need to do is find a way to unwind each day. You may find that you can unwind in the bath or you might want to think about taking a yoga class.

The bad part about life is that usually it's not the major things that make us be unhappy, but it's the little things that can set you back. You need to learn how to be happy, but also how to let go. We can't control the big things and we can't control most little things. Why get uptight about anything that you can't control if there is something that you can't do. Some people have issues with control and when they loss it, they tend to become full of negative feelings. To find your inner peace you have to learn how to unwind and turn the negative feelings into something positive. You will want to do some activities to help you with this.

First, have you ever gotten a message 'have you ever done yoga'? When it comes to the message aspect, you will find that your muscles will loosen up and all the tensions will go away. This may be expensive, but if you can, go at least once a month. Either in the beginning of the month, to let go of last month, or you need to go at the end of the month to prepare for another. If you can, you should go once a week to let go of all the tension.

There is so much stress and tension in some people's lives that you may end the weekly session. Usually you will get a discount from being a regular. Another thing is that you can get a specific message to turn your energy from a negative to a positive one. It's called Reikki. This type of message is where the therapist will take away your negative energy and replace it with their positive energy. It is an incredible thing to do and you will feel 100 times better about yourself as soon as you get up. If a message is not what you'd like, you may want to go and take a yoga class.

Yoga has been proven to help people with their issues. It is claimed that it will turn your negative energy into a positive energy and you will feel refreshed and energized from the class. They teach you how to become in touch with your life and body. Yoga helps a person unwind from all the stress of your work, your family, and everything else. Both Reikki and Yoga have been used for centuries to help a person find inner peace. They both come from a huge background of diversity and has been used by many celebrities to help them unwind from the daily grind.

The whole point of finding inner peace is so that you can live a better life. Your life will be filled with happiness, love, and harmony when you find inner peace. The only thing is that you have to set some time aside to find the inner peace and you will need to be able to let go and allow yourself to be out of control. Once you stop trying to control everything, your life will become peaceful.

How to Learn to appreciate nature

How can you appreciate nature? There are plenty of ways to appreciate nature, but you should use it to your advantage. You should learn how to appreciate the beauty and intelligence of nature. Everyone in nature seems to know their place and they have no complaints. They are so content with themselves, it's hard to see a bear depressed because he's a bear, but nature is so different than what humans is use to. Humans are always wondering about their lives and where they belong.

When you take a walk to the park, sit down, and watch everyone go past you. You should notice the squirrels, the rabbits, and all the other animals and watch how they react to their surroundings. Immediately they will know what to do. You should use that for inspiration. If they know deep in their heart what their role in life is, why can't you? Sit there and watch for a while. Then close your eyes and think about everything that comes so natural to you and you will find your role in life will be just that. Everything that comes natural to you is a part of your true role in life. That's something to think about.

Go for a walk and notice how nature changes to adjust to the environment. The spring, the leaves grow back and then in the summer plants flower, and then in the fall they change once again. They change naturally and it doesn't affect them. That's something to think about also. Change doesn't affect nature, why should you be stressed about it? Change is natural and it is something that happens every couple months. We change in relationships, friendships, work, home, everything can change. You should learn how to except the change and use nature as support. Look at the leaves change and fall. Maybe you're going through a change and you will find ups and down in life. With the bad comes the good, and change is never a bad thing. You can learn and grow from change.

You know what nature also does, it adapts quickly to the changes. Have you ever transplanted a plant? It still grew to be strong and beautiful. This is because nature doesn't worry or fret. Sometimes you will find that you are so stressed out from all the change in your life, but if you think about everything individually, is there anything worth the worry? Humans can adapt to anything just like anything else in nature. If you lose a job, you automatically cut back on savings. If you purchase home, you may adapt by making it your special place. We adapt so quickly to some change, and then wallow about other changes. If only you could adapt to everything and learn how to make a positive out of every negative, you would find your life would be a whole a lot better. You'd be able to enjoy your life if you didn't worry so much.

However, there are times when you need to enjoy your life and nature without having to reflect on it. If you find yourself stressed, you can go out for a walk or to the park and watch the world pass you by. You will see so much on a walk and it can be calming and peaceful. Nature should be embraced in your life because there is so much to learn and nature has it all figured out. All life's important questions can be found on a walk on a path or even around the block. You can find comfort in nature and you can find yourself by appreciating nature.

How to find individual power within

It's hard to find individual power within yourself. There has to be a lot of focus and you have to really want something. When it comes to tragedies and unfortunate events, you wonder how you will ever make it, but you always do. Why? The individual power that you have is used, but also because others support you. There is a difference between making it and making it on your own. When you are making it, you're a complete, but you find the strength to get up out of bed every day for those who need you.

If you have to make it through some thing on your own, you're a bigger mess than ever, but you still seem to carry on. Some people find that their individual power, in this case, comes from responsibility, from others who are supportive, and from your own personal strength. However, sometimes your personal strength is not enough to keep your life from moving forward. You need to find your individual power, but if you don't have the support and responsibilities for others, then you don't have what it takes to pick up the pieces. You don't have a reason to.

Now to find the power within yourself to achieve something, that is much different. Our needs and wants are so strong, they are inspiring and motivational. You can achieve your goals on individual power; however, you have to really want it. When it comes down to it, the person who wins is the one who wants it. If you want, you'll get it. So they key is to not beat yourself for going for something and losing it, because you tried your best and sometimes there are going to be times when you come in second.

It's okay to be second, because that's pure honesty. You'll get first when you find something that you are passionate about and fills your hours with joy. This can be work, a competition, a family, anything that you truly want more than anyone you'll get, because others will see the passion and commitment that you have. When it comes to jobs, passion and commitment is a must.

Change, it's not always welcomed, but everyone has to somehow. What about change? It takes a lot of personal strength for you to deal with change. For change, you find the inner strength within you because of your ambitions and support from others. You will find yourself adapting, because you have the support. You have love around you and you have the support of others to help you find the strength. Moving for the first time is rough. It's scary and you don't know what your life will be like. The key to getting over it is by having support from your family and friends. They will help you with your transition and you will find the strength to be okay. There are thousands of more examples, but you just find your inner strength.

The truth is, there is no way to find your inner strength. It finds you. When you come to a situation where you have to make a choice and both of them are not what you want, you automatically choose the best option for yourself. Your inner strength just seems to pop out. You don't have to worry about muttering up the strength to make a decision. It all comes very natural to everyone. You just seem to find it when you need it. Even if you're scared, somehow, you still find the strength to make your move and save yourself. You'll have the strength from within when you need it.

How to find individual power through religion and beliefs

When it comes to individual power, you have the support of others, your responsibilities, and your moral or religious beliefs. Everyone thinks that religion is what causes so much. People think that you don't need to have a religion anymore, but the truth is, that you get your morals and ethics from your beliefs. You find your individual power through your religion. Without religion, we would have no right and wrong. We wouldn't have any clue to what to do when a serious situation arises. Religion is what guides us through life. It is the basis of society. So how do you find the power through religion?

The answer simple: we find individual power through religion and prayer. When it comes to dealing with matters of death and disease, many people will turn to religion to help them through and understand. Holding on to a high divinity makes everyone feel better. They find strength from knowing that it is part of a plan. They find strength through acceptance. Religions helps a person accept their fate. Not only will comfort you in your time of need, but religion will also comfort those who love you.

When you pray to God sometimes you don't get an answer back, but when you need the strength to make it, you find an answer. When you pray for strength, you can feel someone holding you. It is the spirit inside of you that is comforted and suddenly you feel like a weight has been lifted.

Have you ever read the poem known as Footprints? It says that in good times, there were two sets of footprints. Meaning, in good times God walked beside you. But then the man noticed that in bad times, there was only one set. It angered the man to think that he was alone through all the bad times, but the answer God gave him was that He carried him through the rough times. When you use your religion to help you through the bad times, you can truly believe that God helps you through.

Now what about those who aren't Christian based religions? Religion is different to everyone, but it all has the same job. Your religion will help you through the bad times and help guide you to righteousness when it comes to the good times. It will help you carry on and find strength and support. If you're Jewish, Buddhist, Muslim, or believe in the Greek or Roman gods, you still focus on a higher power to show you the path. Your religion helps you by supporting you in your time of need. Knowing that you are supported will fill you with strength. They are so many religions in the world, but they are tend to support you through the bad and to help guide you to righteousness. It doesn't matter what God you pray to, as long as you have something to believe in.

For those who don't have anything to believe in, there are very unfortunate. The beliefs of religion are the basis of moral and ethical standards that we have. For those who don't believe in anything, they don't have anyone or anything carrying them through the hard times. They have nothing to lean on. They are lost, because, they have to find it on their own. Finding your inner strength is hard, but it's harder when you have nothing pushing you. Religion helps push you to get through things and it helps relieve your pain. You have something to comfort you when bad times happen. There's a reason for everything and believing that it is a higher act of Glory relieves some of the "what if's".

How to realize its not what you believe but that you believe

The key to life is your religion; however, there is so much hype over what you believe that people have forgotten the purpose of believing. It doesn't matter what you believe, but that you believe. There are so many wars in the name of religion, but you lose the sight of your religion when you attack another. Being raised catholic, you will be told that your religion is the only true religion, in fact, all religions say that. You know why?

They need the membership, to be quite honest. How can you call yourself a Christian, when you put down another person because of their religion. When it comes to Christianity, it is a religion that believes in one God and Jesus Christ. There are Methodists, Baptists, Catholics, Orthodox, and more that all believe in God and J.C., however, they criticize each other. Who cares about the small details of what happens and how in the bible! They all believe about the same end. In the end, a Christian will either go to hell or heaven. We all share the same fate, but because of a title, some feel superior to others.

Some people don't have a Christian based religion, however, they all have a religion that states what's right and wrong. All religions have a basis of the same right and wrongs, and that is why we have general laws in our states and countries. When it comes to religion, if you follow the belief, you will find your haven. Knowing that there is a place after life that you will go and enjoy your afterlife is the reason why we feel empowered by religion. Everyone has a different haven or variety of heaven, but it's the goal of all humanity.

Our religions help us find the strength to follow our path of righteousness to find the safe haven after life. It doesn't matter the details of your life, religion, or after life, what matters is that you made the most out of it. What matters is that when you were down on your knees, there was a divine power inside of you that allowed you to carry on. This divine power helped you and carried you in your time of need and you got through the rough times.

If you don't believe in anything, you will never know what it feels like to be empowered. You will never know what it feels like to be truly supported.

Religion is one of the hardest things for people to get over, but as long as you believe, then you should never let anyone take that away from you. In fact, when you believe, you are empowered with a divine light that stays inside of you. No one can ever take that away from you. You'll always have someone or something inside you to help you through the craziness of life and through the best times of your life.

Going back to Christianity, have you ever read the poem Footprints? In the poem God walks along side of a man in the best times of his life. In the best times he saw two footprints in the sand. When times got rough, there was only one. When the man asked God why he left him, God responded by saying," During your times of trial and suffering, When you see only one set of footprints, it was then that I carried you." You will find that in any religion, with any God, that this is true. In your time of need, your religion will help carry you to the safe haven and you will find the strength to carry on and the strength to follow a high moral life.

How to keep the mind busy to explore your intelligence levels

Do you like a good challenge? Some people like a challenge and others prefer to go the safe journey through life, however, if you explore your intelligence, not only will you expand your mind, but you will find things out about yourself that you never knew. You will find that you are stronger than you think. You will find that you have the power to achieve things that are completely out of your reach by finding the power inside of yourself. If you can keep your mind busy you can add years and years to your life. The knowledge allows you to grow.

Another key point to keeping the mind busy is that you can keep going. Most people who retire and then don't have a hobby or just get older, tend to go quickly because they didn't keep their mind stimulated. If you can, you should try to find ways to keep your mind stimulated throughout your years.

You should do puzzles, get a hobby, do crosswords, anything that will stimulate your mind and your intelligence. You need to constantly keep your mind in good use or you will find that you will lose some of your mind. In fact, many older adults find that they develop mental incapability because they just stopped doing things after retirement. They didn't go out and purchase word puzzle books or puzzles. They just sort of watched TV and didn't do much. To keep yourself young and alive you need to do things that will stimulate your mind.

Not only will it keep you young and vibrant, but it will also help you to discover your intellect levels. If you can do puzzles and everything as a hobby, you will find that your mind will think quicker and you'll have all this extra knowledge that you never knew you had. You will tap into a large amount of knowledge from having to solve all the puzzles. Your mind will think quickly and process the knowledge quickly for you to come to a conclusion quickly. You will find that your mind will be sharper than anyone else if you keep your mind stimulated. However, you have to take some breaks. Your mind needs some rest. So you can't finish a puzzle that's thousands of pieces a day, however, if you can spend some of your time, an hour or two a day, working and stimulating your mind, you will find a vast improvement in your mental capabilities.

Another thing that you can do is keep yourself physically active. If you can stay active and do some excise, you mind will be effected. Exercise has been proven to help people with depression and other mental disturbances, as well as, relieve things like stress and anxiety. If you can let go of all of that, you will find that you can remember things better and your mind will become healthy. It's like reliving of it from carrying all the stress and burdens that it may have. The key to living long is to keep your mind healthy and to keep your body healthy. You can't do one or the other, you must do both. It can be hard for some to do this, but with discipline you should be able to.

You should care about your mind and your health at a very young age. If you can keep yourself active and expanding on your intellect levels, you will be able to add years on to your life and you will find a way to live a healthy and happy life. It is very important for you to keep yourself healthy.

How to Learn to love even if you feel you never can

How do you know that you are in love or even like someone? You may find that the object of your affection is opposite of what you look for and may not be that attractive compared to Brad Pit (but most aren't). However, you still may find yourself wanting to spend time with them and fall in love. The only thing is when you fall in love, you don't want to love for love. You want to love because you are in love. Love can begin with the oddest circumstances and bloom into a lasting and passionate romance.

What is love? You know, love is the most awkward word to define. By a dictionary, you will find that it is a "profound feeling of affection and attraction". However, what is it? Love can not be described because it is different for everyone, but you know when you are in love. You feel a deep passion for them. You miss them every time they leave. You have an emotional, romantic, and desire to be with them as a supporter, as a friend, and as a lover. It can be complex. Love is painful and love and pleasurable. Love is everything rolled into one word. You seem to lose all sense of time and logic when you are in love. When it comes to love and logic, the heart always wins.

IF you think that you are in love, you need to do all you can to save that feeling. You need to proceed in the relationship with caution. You may have been hurt before, or you may never have felt this before and it's something that you need to be cautious. Although love is never a guarantee, you can love and trust someone who deserves it and is worthy of your love. You should talk to your interest and tell them how you feel and how you would like to pursue the relationship, but with hopes that your feelings will be taken inconsideration of. Everyone hurts someone that they love deeply once or twice.

Even the most solid relationships have rocky times, but the key is to finding a mutual understanding to help preserve your feelings. Even if the relationship ends, you can always think about how true the love was and that it was a miracle for you to truly find love. Many people go through out their entire lives without finding true love. You should consider yourself lucky.

When it comes to love, you have ot start off slowly. Don't rush things! You have all the time in the world and love always seems to stop time. Don't rush your love or relationship into serious matters like marriage or even an engagement. It will happen with time. Don't rush into things because you need to know that you feel is love and not lust. If you find yourself completely in awe before you even have relations then you are most likely in love, but if the first thing you want to do is have sex, then your in lust. There is no love in lust, but you can find a healthy sexual relationship in love. Some times it can be confusing, but you know when you are in love.

If you would do anything for someone, even lay your life on the line for him or her, you're in love. If you are a tough guy and you find a woman who can bring you to your knees or cry, then you're in love. When you are willing to go the extra mile for them, you're in love. Everyone can love and some will love, but you may end up finding love in the last place you would think.

How to Learn to get past the pain and find life

It's hard to get over the past when yours is filled with pain and lost love. You need to get over the past and focus on the future and the life that you can have. There are a lot of people are new to the dating and scene and things might have changed since you were last single, but if you take your time and not eager to rush things, you can find serious love again. First, you should not wait for Mr. Perfect. Mr. Perfect really doesn't exist anymore in life. There is no such thing so stop waiting. You need to go out with people who have an interest in you, and that you have an interest in. Even if you don't like the person, you still might want to accept a date so that you can get some practice and get back in the game.

After one date, you don't have to continue it. You don't have to rush a first date either. If the date is going well, you still should be cautious about taking the date to another level. You might want to wait awhile before you start the sexual relations because you have been hurt before and you don't want to place your trust in the wrong person, especially, if you are just starting to date again.

You need to get back out there. Go to a club, art show, and anywhere else that you can image connection with someone, even if it is your best friend. You don't have to go alone either. If you have a friend, you will feel more comfortable to be yourself. If you can be yourself then you will be more comfortable when it comes to a first date. So as you can see, everything you do will have an effect on something. Just take things one day at a time. If you can take things one day at a time you will find that things will come easy.

Then once you start dating, don't do anything exclusive. You should go on several first dates, before you go out on a second. You need to "shop around" before you get serious. If you have been out of the game for awhile, you will want to be cautious of serious relationships. You don't want to get burned again. Also, if you aren't exclusive, then you have no fear of being rejected because you have plenty of more people.

What do you do if you find someone who you really like, but you just got out of this terrible relationship and not sure about getting into another? Well, explain to the person about your situation and the way that you feel about love and dating. Be honest and direct. If you aren't sure about a relationship then tell them that you want to take things slowly and just see what happens. It might bloom, it might not. However, you shouldn't allow the doubt to get in way of your fun. Clearly tell them that you have a lot fun and wouldn't want to miss out on more. This way they really know that you're just not sure.

When it comes to love and pain, you love, you live, and then you learn. You should reflect on your other relationships and learn from them. You'll learn what to do and what not to do in a relationship. If you had an abusive or horrible relationship, you know what signs to look out for and you know getting out early is best. You should never compare someone to an ex, because they are very different, however, when it comes to abuse, they are all the same.

How to remember and find that everything does happen for a reason

When it comes to the good things in life we always say because of hard work and determination. Then, when it comes to the bad things in life, it was just meant to be. Why is there such a double standard? Everyone happens, and it happens for a reason. There are so many things that will determine your life and your destination.

One of those reasons is pre-destination. There are a lot of people who have a religion or just believe that we are all effects from pre-destination. From the moment we are born, our lives are planned to every detail. We are born with a pre-destination that states how lives will be and where we will end up. Pre-destination has been an ancient way of thinking. For centuries, people believed that it didn't matter about the little things that happened in our lives because we had a destiny and you can't avoid destiny. That's one reason why things happen.

As for the Christian way, things happen for a divine reason. There are times when God takes a life because you were pure and ready for heaven. Bad things happen to good people because God allowed it to happen. God allowed it to happen because the person was ready. They were as good as they would ever be and ready to go to his kingdom. Then they claim that bad things happen to bad people because of karma. In the bible, you are to treat your peers as you would like to be treated, and if not, then you'll get it back three times. So bad things happen because of the old saying, "What goes around comes around."

As for the true reason for why things happen, you'll never know. The only way that you can have comfort in the fact those things happen for a reason is if you have a religion or belief. If you have a religion you can find comfort in your beliefs, but it's so hard to believe that there was a reason why bad things happen to good people.

It's so hard to blame someone, especially, God for something like that. It's hard to believe that God would allow you to feel so much pain in the world, but there is a reason. With the pain, comes to the happiness. You have to go through pain to appreciate what you have. To appreciate who you are and what you have experienced, you have to have some sorrow. The hard times is what brings people closer, and it also, brings you to recognize the truth and honesty.

You may say that you hate someone and that you wish you never knew them, but the moment they are gone, you sit and cry. You had to loose what you had to realize what you had. When it comes to a lesson, people believe that God teaches value lessons, but there is no lesson. There is just a time for some and a time for others. God is a merciful God and He doesn't do things for spite. Don't blame God for things that happen, but reflect on the fact that he has a plan. You may not understand the plan, but there is a plan.

There is no excuse that you should use to find comfort. There is no way that you will ever understand why things happen, but you should know that one day you'll know why. You will find comfort in your religion and belief, as well as, the support of those around you. Everything happens for a reason; however, you may never know the reasoning behind anything.

Why do you feel it happened to you? And what you can do to change it

There are a lot of things that you may feel happened to you for no reason. The first thing that you will want to ask yourself is how this happened and why you. The truth is there is nothing you can to change it, however, there are things that you can do to help yourself and your family cope. When it comes to bad things, there are many things that you say you wish you did, but you can't go back and relive it.

There is no point on going over the "what ifs", because you can't change anything. If you can't change anything, then why wallow. You may not be able to change the way you feel for a long time and that's okay. You need to allow yourself the grieving time and you should allow yourself the anger and the emotions. Then, you need to be able to find support in friends and family and then try to move on.

The only thing that you can do is to help everyone cope with the changes that lives has made. If you loose someone very dear to you, don't get bitter. It's not what they would have wanted from you. What you should do is ask them for help and strength to carry on. Remember, just because you lost someone doesn't mean it's forever. Eventually everyone meets everyone again and things are easier if you think like that. There is no reason for you to buddle everything up and cut them out of your life. You have your family and friends and you have your memories.

Memories are very important. They are what keep us strong. When we get lonely, all that is needed is a cup of a tea and a photo album. Comfort is found in the memories. If you cut yourself off from everything that reminds you, you would not be doing justice for them. It may be easier to forget, but it's still hard to forgive. There are some people who would not want you to forget them, but forgive for the sake of others. You should talk to others about their feelings about loss and try to comfort them. You should try to keep in mind that their spirit is alive and well.

Although you are so quick to judge and blame someone, there is no one to blame in acts like this. If there was carelessness, you won't feel any better about the accident if you push for a conviction. You should not try to get revenge. First of all, it's not healthy, and second, it won't bring back the life that you lost. To carry on, it's hard when you lost someone dear to you. However, you should think about all those people who would be affected by your revenge. It won't make you feel better and sure won't write anything.

Leave the justice up to the courts and be okay with the ruling, regardless of what it may be. Also, don't blame yourself or others for the loss. You can't beat yourself down because you didn't pick up on signs or you didn't stay with them that night.

When they are sick for some time, for a moment, there is comfort in their death. They don't suffer anymore. Then you feel horrible because you thought that. The truth is, no one knows why things happen and why only certain people are affected. You never know what live will hand you, but you must make the best of it. Always remember and forget, but there is a time when you need to forgive and let go.

How to live with the spirit of others in life

There are many things in life that we have to deal with. Sometimes, we may feel like we are in another world floating around. We may feel like we are not the people that we want to be because of the influence of others around us. We want to make sure that we are finding a way to be ourselves so that we can live a happy and successful life.

There are many people around us that may influence the way that we feel. Sometimes the people around us can be real life people that we see and talk to. They may be people that try and take over the way that we act and feel. It is sometimes hard to make these people understand that we have to live out our own life and do the things that make us happy.

If there are not real life people hanging around, there are spirits lurking that will put a lot of persuading on the way that we act and feel. There may be someone that is deceased and no longer in this life, but you may feel his or her presence around you at the same time. You may feel like they are there among all the thoughts and decisions that you make in life trying to give you advice for one reason or another.

Finding out what you want and who you are in life is not always easy. Sometimes there is just too much pressure from the people around us when it comes to who we want to be and what we want to do. When there are too many spirits interacting with our daily lives and trying to give advice, it can be overwhelming and a little bit frustrating at the same time. It is hard to find a way to go on in life and not have to do what others want us to.

We have to be strong willed and move along in life with our own strength. We need to find our passions and go with the flow. When there is something that we feel strong about and we want to do more than anything in life, we need to go after it and make the dreams that we once had come true. There is no need to do what everyone else wants us to all the time. We need to push past the things that are difficult and listen to the advice that other spirits around us give, but in the end, it is our decision to make. We need to listen to our inner spirits and go after the things that we feel good about.

Having spirits around us that try to give us help and comfort when we need it is a great thing. There are many people that turn to these spirits for the safe feeling that they are looking for. There is nothing wrong with wanting to feel secure and safe, however we need to make our own decisions and go with what we believe is right. When we are strong and dependable, we will find a way to make anything happen.

Living with the spirits of others in life is something that we can adjust to. We do not have to push everyone out of our way. In fact we should feel some sort of comfort in knowing that we have people that love us and want to take care of us. When we have this secure feeling, we will have a much better chance at living a fulfilling life and be much happier from the inside out.

If you don't like your life, change it and how to

Many of us do not like how we are living our life. We may find that we are not happy with the choices that we make and things that are going on in our life right now. When this is the case, we must try and find ways to make our life better. We cannot just sit back and let these unwanted things stay in our life. We will not be happy and we risk living a very unsatisfying life.

Having a positive attitude in life is something that will get you a good start at changing your life. You will want to have great thoughts of success and happiness. You need to lose the feelings of depression and defeat. Life is about being happy and upbeat. You can expect to get further in life when you are going at it with great thoughts and a positive outlook on life.

There are many things that we can do to help change our life. When we find that we are in a rut and not happy with some of the things in our life, we need to make the necessary changes to make them better. We can do this by putting a little bit of effort and thought into the process. There are so many opportunities and if we have our eyes shut, we may miss them.

The first thing that we need to do is find out what is making us unhappy. We must make a plan to figure out what is bringing our life down so bad. Once we find the reason, we can then start to make the changes and once again feel good about whom we are and what we are doing. This is very important because we need to establish some type of plan so that we are able to make our dreams and goals in life a reality.

If you are not happy with your job or career path, it is time to change it. There is no rule stating that you have to be one thing for the rest of your life. You will find that there are many opportunities out there and all you need is the drive to move forward and go after what you want. You do not have to earn all the money in the world to be happy. If you are not getting the satisfaction from your career that you want, you may find that it is time for a career change to something that brings you the feeling of accomplishment and gratitude.

If you are lonely in life because you are not with a significant other, you may want to start thinking about how you can change it. You may want to find someone that you can share your life with. This does not have to be a romantic relationship. It can be someone that you enjoy spending time with whether it is for a night on the town or just sitting in front of the television watching movies. You need to find someone that you can share your stories with and confide all your most private details with. This person can be a new friend or a close relative as long as you feel comfortable sharing with them.

When your life is not as you expected, you do not have to just sit there and take it. You need to find a way to get back on track. Life is too short to just sit and watch it go by. You need to find something that makes you happy and thrilled about being alive. This can be anything that you want. You can make it a hobby that you love or the car that you drive. It makes no difference what bring fun and excitement to your life. It is the fact that you are taking advantage of it and making the thrill of life happen for you.

How to realize nothing is going to be given to you but you have to work for it

It is important for us to realize that nothing in life that is worth anything is given to us for free. We need to understand that we have to work for the things in life that we want and need. There are so many things that we would like to have, but it is important to see that you have to work for them and be willing to make your dreams and life goals come true.

When we are young, we are taken care of by those around us. We have our friends, family and parents to help us along. We are protected and given things that we want. However, it is very valuable to learn that we are not always going to get what we want. We have to realize that things in life are not free and from there we have to find a way to get them.

When you learn from a young age that we have to work for what we want, we will make life changes to find a way to make them happen. We may have to work a little bit harder and wait for them, however the feeling that you get when you get something on your own is outstanding. There is nothing better in the world than the feeling of accomplishment. It is something that we all want to achieve and have felt at some point in our life.

Getting what we want from a job or career is something that we have to be willing to work for too. We may have to do a little more research and some more studying to get the dream career that we have always wanted. This life that we want and dream about is not just going to happen because we want it to. There are certain things that you need to do on your own to make them a reality.

If you are someone that wants to have the better things in life and loves to have materialistic items you may find that you are no longer going to get them handed to you. Why should you? No one will like having things handed to them forever because it means that you do not have the courage and the self-respect to go after what you have always wanted. You need to stand on your own and make the life changes that are necessary to get to where you want to be.

Making sure that you are happy is one of the most important things that you can do for yourself. You will want to be sure that you are allowing yourself to achieve the goals that you have worked hard for. You will want to be someone that you can be proud of every time you get something that you need or want. You will feel great and more alive because you did what you have to in order to go after what you want.

Finding out what you want in life is not something that will come to easily. You may have to wait and work hard at it. You may have to struggle for a bit because you are not able to find out everything all at once. You might have to take your time and find out who you are from the inside out. Once you do this, you are going to be able to find the strength and the courage to get something for yourself. This is something that you can be proud of and continue to do each day.

Changing others by showing them how to set goals

Goals are one of the most important things in life. You will want to have goals for each step of the way. Some people set long-term goals, however it is just as important to have short-term goals that you can achieve as well. You will have the power to set your own personal and business goals and then do what you need to so that they are followed through on.

If you are someone that has goals and uses them to make their life better, you may want to help others achieve goals as well. This is something that you can do and feel great about because you are giving someone else the power to make choices for their own life and have positive goals that they can feel good about.

You can change the way that other people think about life when you show them the importance of setting goals. You will be able to show them that they can make great efforts to get to where they want to be and soon see them pay off. It is a great feeling to help someone else and by showing him or her how to set goals and follow through on them, you will be lending a great hand to them.

You can show your children how to set goals and follow up on them. You will want to teach your children or a child that is close to you how to set important goals in life. You can show them this from a very young age. This is some thing that will help them throughout life. They will see how setting goals can change their life for the better. It will make them more responsible and more perceptive to what life has to offer them.

As a child learns about goals and setting them, they can do this for everyday. Making the bed, doing their homework, and learning a new song are just a few things that a child can set as goals for themselves on a daily basis. For the more long-term goals, they can stride to get good grades, make more friends or get more exercise. These are all great examples of how they can make their life better by setting realistic goals that can help them with life and things that happen in it.

Once you get to adult life, you will see that goals are very crucial to being mature. You will find that being mature means that you have to be willing to set your goals and make standards for yourself. Once you do this, you will see that you can do more for your self-esteem and for your character. Being someone that has goals and wants to do better with every step of the way will change them into the person that they want to become.

There is nothing wrong with not knowing what you want as your goals in life. Not everyone has it all planned out. There are many people that are confused and may have a hard time finding themselves. When this is the case, they will want to think a little more about their goals and try to find ways to meet them as time goes.

Do not set goals that are outrageous. All this will do is set you up for a huge fall. You will want to make your goals something that you know you can achieve even over time. You may need longer to get there, but you will find the person that you want to be through them.

How to change your own life by learning to suppress negative spirits

We all have feelings and spirits inside us. We may not be able to explain some of the feelings that we have, but it is important to find ways to keep them under control. There are plenty of things that make us unhappy. We may not always be as happy and cheerful as we would like to be. It is very normal to have negative thoughts and spirits inside. However, we have to find ways to suppress them when we can.

You can change your life when you are finding ways to suppress your negative spirits. You will not want to let them overwhelm your life. You want to have good feelings too. There are ways that you can help to make the bad turn into good so that you are able to be happier and live a more productive life. You will feel better and find the presences around you to be happier and healthier as well.

You can start by finding out whom you are and what you want to do. When you are sure of the person that you want to become, you will find it much easier to live a well thought out life. You will have everything planned out in front of you so that you are able to make the most of your life and what you want from it. You can suppress the bad feelings and bring out the good spirits that you know are in there.

Another way to help change the negative to the positive is to have good thoughts. You will want to make sure that you are always thinking about good thoughts. You will want to be happy and think about the good things in life. This will put you in a zone of pleasant and wonderful feelings on both the inside and the outside. You will then start to show these feelings of positive thoughts and use them in a positive way. This will give you more power to succeed in life too.

Exercise and rest are two important things to getting rid of the negative spirits that are hidden inside of you. You will want to get as much exercise as you can on a regular basis. You will want to find a routine and get going with it. When you are planning out your routine, you will be able to keep on track and this will help you loose those unwanted spirits as well as help get your body in shape too.

Rest is one of the most important things when it comes to good thoughts. You will want to be sure that you are sleeping well at night so that you are allowing your body to rest and to feel like you want it to. You do not want to have bad feelings taking over your body because you have so much tension and stress overriding you. You will actually feel better when you are allowing your body to take the time off that it deserves and you will have better thoughts and positive spirits too.

You can think about the things in your life that bring negative spirits to your life. This can be anything from a certain person to a job. You may want to find a way to relieve your body of these negative things and put more positive forces in it. You will want to use good spirits to make your life happier and healthier. You will feel better more and more as you go because you are putting more positive energies into your life. This is something that is well worth the thought behind it.

How to realize there is another world after death

If you are not sure what happens to you after your body has died, you may want to do some research. There are many theories to this question, but does anyone really know what happens? You cannot be sure because anyone that has already died will be the only ones to know. We will not be able to find out the real truth until our passing time comes. However, there are ways to find out what may or may not happen to the soul of humans when death occurs.

There are many people that believe that your body is the only thing that is left when you are deceased. They believe that your soul and mind are gone and have already been accepted by the good or the evil spirits. It is something that many religions over time have thought about and you may want to read into it a little bit more before you come up with an actual decision about what you believe.

For some, there is no right or wrong. They believe that your soul is going to float around and not be taken by any spirits. You will be lingering around the world and trying to have a peaceful and everlasting life. However, you are only a spirit so how can you actually have a life when you cannot be seen, taste, touch and speak to those that you once loved in your former life.

Another theory in the life after death sequence is that your soul is transferred to another body. You will be someone else in a different life. You may never have any recollection of your former life, but you may find that some things seem similar like you have already done them before. This is when you are reincarnated into a different world that is much different from the life that you had before. You may or may not feel changed, but regardless your spirit is changed because of the new environment that you are now living in.

Some believe yet another theory and that is that you are either entered into the gates of hell or the castle of heaven. Many religions preach that when you are an evil spirit and you have done bad things in your life, you will be punished for eternity in the persecution of hell. This is not the recommended place to go for most Christians. Many of them work hard at saving their soul and getting forgiveness for their sins so that they can enter the beauty of the Lords Kingdom in heaven one day. This is the destination chosen for the good spirits that have lived a life of greatness and goodness.

There are so many things that you may or may not believe will happen to you when you are no longer alive and your body has passed. Your soul is believed to live on and go onto another form. It is believed to most that there is some sort of live after death and that it is as good or even better than life on earth is for most before they die. It is all about waiting and determining who was really right and what really does happen to us when we die.

The main thing is to know that there is something waiting for us all after death. We have to realize that this wonderful world is not over when we die. Things will still go on and people will also go on with their daily lives. We have to realize that there is another world out there for the deceased and it may or may not be something far more wonderful than what we have ever imagined.

How to create functions that make you a part of a group

It is not always easy being accepted into a group. You may feel left out and lonely at times. It is hard to make everyone like you and to fit into every part of life. It can sometimes be frustrating and hard to deal with especially when you want so much to fit into somewhere and you want others to like you so much.

You will find that you can try and do a few things to make others let you fit in as a group. You can try and do a few of these things so that you are noticed and well liked in the event that you want to be part of the group but you are not sure what you can do to make them want you. It may be rough at times, but with a little persuasion and some hard work, you can make it happen.

You can make your very own function so that you are more likely to fit in. You can commit to your own group of people so that you are able to fit in better with a group. You can make up your own rules so that you will find others that will be great for your group. You will feel better because you are able to fit into the group better. You will see that there are many people that will come to or join your group so that you can show them that you are fun and that you belong to their group.

Being part of a group is something that everyone wants to do. We all want to be liked and have fun with our friends. We want to get out there and meet new people and fit into the group so that we are better able to meet friends and get along with others. Everyone wants to do this and they want to become part of a social group so that they can raise their self-esteem and grow.

You need to be open. You should be able to meet new people and make conversation. You will want to be able to talk to others and open up as a person. You will want to be ready for the challenge of greeting others and participating in a group. This is all part of joining a group and actually becoming part of it. You will want to be involved and create other functions that you all can do as a group. You may want to choose something that you know about so that you can help the others if they are in need. You will look better and be part of the group more when you are able to become part of the fun.

It is going to take a while for you to make friend and become part of the group as you want. It may take longer than what you think, however if you have the patience and are willing to go after what you want, you will see that it can payoff for you and this can be a great time. Your group will learn to see the fun and the good in you and they will want you to be part of them as much as you want to become a member in their group.

Do not get frustrated. It can happen for you and in fact if you wait long enough, you can have the group that you want and feel good. You will see that you can be part of a group and find friendship and fun that you have been waiting for.

How to feel more alive by fulfilling your need to be a part of anything

Being part of something is important. We all want to feel like we belong. This may be something that we have to work for and it may not come to us overnight. We need to make the most of our life and do the things that we want to in order to be happy. We all want to feel more alive. This is what fulfills our lives and gives us the need to go on in life.

We all want to be accepted. We all want to feel like we belong and that other people like us. This is part of life. We have to find ways to make our life count and how to fulfill the needs and the wants in our life. We deserve to live life like we want and to feel more alive with each day. This is very important so that we all are able to make our dreams of being accepted in this world a little bit easier.

We have to make the most of each day and make it happen for us. This may be something that we have to work a little harder at, but we have to stride for better things. It is something that may or may not be hard for most of us, but it is well worth it in the end. You will feel like you are being accepted as part of a group so that you are able to go on and feel good about being there.

You can join any type of group. This can be anything from a sports team to a special group. You can join something that makes you happy and allows you to take part in the things that you like. This is very important and will give you the feeling of belonging and being part of a particular group. You will feel more special and this in turn will lift your spirits and give you the outlook on life that you want for the best life possible.

You will see that from a young age, being part of a group is very important. You may want to join a group when you are in school and this will carry on with your throughout life. You will learn that you will need to try and fit in even at an early age. You will see that you can be part of any group that you feel encouraged by. If you want to play sports, join a club that involves your favorite hobby, or do something that challenges you, you can be part of the group so that you are able to live a happier and well-rounded life.

You will be part of a group as long as you are willing to participate in the functions and stride to do better in your life. You will see that others will accept you and want you to be part of their life. This will be something that you can do for yourself to help your self-esteem and to make you feel like you are accepted in life. You will see that this can help to improve your life and your way of thinking. You can increase your energy and even improve your health when you are willing to give it your all and make the most of your life. You can certainly use this group to make your life better and to give you the self-respect that you are looking for.

How to open your spirit and learn more about the feelings of others

We all have to be compassionate to others. It may be hard at times to think about how others feel, however we need to be aware of their feelings and let them know that we are listening and there for them when needed. It is all part of our spirit and how we can learn about other people by listening to their feelings.

We have to open our hearts and our minds to others. When we have the ability to put others first, this will show that we do care how other people feel and that they are important to us. We need to be aware of how we react to other's feeling so that we are not making them feel bad. We need to be thoughtful and respectful so that they have the respect they deserve from us. We will see that how we treat others will reflect on how others treat us.

We need to open up our spiritual side and let our true feelings flow out. We have to allow our inner side to be free and to move on so that we can have a positive life and be happier people. When someone is down, we need to pick up on that. When someone is feeling happy, we also should reflect on this so that we are not doing anything to ruin this happy feeling. We need to do all that we can to make them feel good and bring more enjoyment to their life.

If someone is not feeling good about something, we should be able to see that. We need to be aware of their feelings and try to find ways to make it better. We need to be there for our friends and make them feel like they are the most important person to you. You will see that you can do better by listening to how they are feeling and trying to find a solution to their problem by understanding what they are going through.

It is very necessary to try and be a better person in every way possible. This may include being more social and finding ways to make more friends. The only way that you can do this is by finding ways to listen to others and allowing their feelings to be important. You will want to make sure that you are doing this so that you are bringing your own life up to expectation. By taking the time to have compassion for others feelings, we will be able lift your own life to the fullest. You will have a better spirit and make the most from your life.

You can read up on how to do this with books. There are plenty of resources out there that will help you find ways to be a better person. You will see how you can react to different problems and how to make them better for you and everyone else involved. You will see that there are lessons to learn and ways to be more attentive to how people are feeling around you. You will want to use these practices and bring more energy to yourself.

You are not going to be able to pick up on these things right away. In fact you will see that you have the right to make your own life choices and by being a better person, you will see that you will in turn have a great experience and be better appreciated by others around you.

When you feel things are bad, think about how bad it could be

There are times when we think to ourselves that life cannot get any worse. However we have to realize that we can have it worse off than what it really is. We should take the time to be appreciative about the things that we do have and not be disappointed about the things that we do not have. We need to make sure that we are able to go on and be able to see that things can get better and in fact they will.

Life has its way of throwing us curve balls and making things hard. This is something that we should realize how to get through and move on past. We do not have to concentrate on the bad things in life; in fact we can focus in on the great things and use this time to improve our way of life and what we do in it. We do not have to accept things the way they are because we as humans have the power to change them for the better.

We all take the hard times bad. At that moment we believe that things are the worst they could be. This is not always true. We need to think ahead and realize that things can actually be much worse and that we should be very thankful for the things that we do have. When we are injured, we think that things are truly bad. However we need to think about the other binaries and how much worse it really could be. We in fact could be dead instead of just injured. We can also recover and we should not think about the bad things that happen and concentrate on the good things.

We need to find ways to think positively. Each day that we are given in life is a precious gift. We have to find ways to be thankful so that we are able to feel good about each moment. We need to be considerate of all the wonderful gifts in our life and take each day as a gift. We will see that when we have this type of attitude in life, we will do better and have a happier and less stressful life. We do not need to add more stress in our life because this is something that will only harm us in the end.

It is very important to have good faith. We need to sit back and be thanking full for all the things in life that we have and not ponder on what we think we think we deserve. If life is busy handing us some hard times, we need to find a way to make them better and to give us a better outlook. There is no sense in going around feeling sorry for feeling or ourselves like we have been handed a bad deal. We need to move past these feelings and find ways to make it better.

It may take some time to improve our life. It may take some hard work and determination as well. However, when we work hard to change the things that make us sad, we will see that we can learn from them and make life a little bit better. It is important to make the most of what we have and keep on going forward. We need to be aware of the things around us that can make us feel down. We need to try and avoid these things so that we are able to stay positive and keep happy thoughts. This is all part of being healthy and making your life better than what you expect. We can have it all and make the most of the things that we have.

Remember it can always be much worse than it is right now.

How to deal with the life you have

We all should realize that life is a precious gift. We need to find ways to be thankful for what we have. There are so many people that take life for granted and do not stop to see the things that they are given and all the happiness that they could have. Life is not always good. This is something that everyone knows. We should not expect to have things handed to us and think about what we can do to make our life better and what we want.

Some will choose to deal with their problems and try to find ways to fix them. This is the best thing that you can do. You do not want to ignore them because all this will do is preserve them for another day. The sooner you deal with your problems; the better off you can expect things to be.

If you are having a hard time dealing with the life that you have, you have to realize that there are things that you can do to change it. You are the only one that has the power to turn your life around. You can make the most from the instances that you are living in and take the time to make each moment count. This is something that will make you sees just what you really do have and that you deserve the best in life.

You can take the necessary steps to make your life what you want. You do not have to wait for life to happen to you. You can have made your life happen for you. Doing this is something that you should take time to think about. You will want to think about what you want to do for your life and what you want out of it. If you are unhappy with your job, relationship, or home, you should take the time to think about what you need to do to change them.

You are in control of the drivers seat in life. You are the only one that knows what you really want and how to get it. There are no excuses for not getting what you want. If you are unsure of how to make things happen for you, you may want to reevaluate your life and try to find out what you are looking for. You may have to switch your career, end a bad relationship, or move to another location to get what you need to be happy. Your happiness is the most important thing in life and you have to do what you need in order to protect it.

You should not give up. Many people think that their life is bad and there is nothing left to do about it. They will do nothing to change it and keep moving forward in the life they have. People will do this even though it is not healthy and it is making them feel bad. It is very crucial to find out what you can do to make your life better and get out of the rut that you are stuck in. You need to move past the feelings of sadness and move on to being happy and getting the life that you deserve.

Do not listen to other people. You only have one life and you will need to make it exactly as you want. You will find that sometimes people try and bring you down. You need to distance yourself from these people and move on to bigger and better opportunities. You deserve to have the best and to have all the advantages that you want in life. This is something that you can do for yourself so that you are living life to the fullest. This is the only way that you are able to make life better so that you can deal with it better.

How your inner spirit gives you strength

Everyone has an inner spirit. This is something that gives us the strength and the help that we are looking for at certain times in our life. We all have times when we need to rely on the help of others. When this time happens, we need to use our inner strength to give us the support that is necessary to get us through. We should listen to this inner spirit and make the most of it when we can.

There are many people that do not realize that we have the inner spirits inside us. When this is the case, we should stop and think about whom we talk to when we are in need and what gives us the feelings of being secure and happy. We should use these feelings and bring them out for when we are confused and when we are in need of some type of help. We can talk to our inner spirits when we are looking for inner strength to rely on.

We have the feelings inside us that tell us right from wrong. We sometimes listen to them and other time we ignore what they are trying to tell us.

This is something that many think of as their self-conscious. It is however, the inner spirits talking to you and helping you find your way. They are there to protect you and help you achieve your life goals by giving you the strength that you need when you need it.

There are times in everyone's life when they are in need of some type of support. They may need emotional or physical support. The one place that we know we can get this help from is our inner strength. We can find the help that we have been looking for and that no one else has right inside of ourselves. This is the way that we can make our dreams come true in life because we have the inner spirits pushing us to make life better and to go on with what makes us happier.

Emotional inner spirits will be there when no one else will. You should lean on them and make them your priority in life. We all know that we have thoughts and feelings about spirits and some believe and others do not. However, it is important to know that you can fulfill your life goals and make them what you want. You do not have to go on in life with no support. You have it with you all the time and some may not even realize it.

There are times when we are faced with making a decision that we are just not sure about. These times can be grueling and we may have to find some help. We can turn to our friends and family for some advice but in the end, it is the inner spirits that give us the help we are after. They are the ones that guide us through when we are confused and unsure of what we should be doing. We are the only ones that can make our life decisions and we need to find the inner strength that we are looking for to make goals and dream a reality.

You can be a better person by bringing out the inner spirit in yourself. You can achieve those hard to reach goals and make your life a better one by taking the time to express how you are really feeling. Letting your inner spirits give you strength is just one way that you can make your life better and a whole lot easier at the same time.

Your inner beliefs do have an impact on people around you

The way that you feel inside and what you believe in is going to have an impact on others. There are things that we do in life that make others feel good or bad depending on what we are doing. We need to try and find a way to make a good impact on how others feel about us and what we can do to make them see that your beliefs are important to you and how you are feeing.

Your inner beliefs are something that can be different from others around you. You need to focus in on what you think is right and what you can do to make people feel good around you. You should not want to hurt anyone because of the things that you believe in. Everyone is different and it is crucial that you know that you cannot push others to be like you or to think the way that you do. It is ok to express your feelings and to be proud of who you are and what you believe in as long as you are not hurting others intentionally.

The way that you feel about things inside will affect the people around you. You will find that there are many vibes that will come off around you. People will sense the good and the bad things and will determine what they think of you and your beliefs. You should make sure that you are considerate and treat others, as you would want to be treated. You should think about what you want to do and how this can make your life better as well as the people that are around you.

There are many inner spirits that you may have. You may have them at different times. You can feel good about certain things and bad about others. It is important to know that you are the only one that can control the way that you live your life. You want to make sure that you are not putting others in danger of getting hurt because of the way that you do things. You want others to have positive experiences when they are around you so that they can be positive and feel good when you are around.

Treating others, as you would want to be treated is a very good line. You should try and keep this important goal at the top of your priority list. You need to do well unto others so that you can in turn feel good about who you are and what you are doing in life.

Your inner beliefs are going to help determine what you do for the rest of your life. You will see that the way you feel on the inside is going to affect the way that you feel on the outside. You want to glow and be happy so that you are able to show this to others. You can make a great impact on the lives of your friends and family when you are willing to show the goodness and the love that you have on the inside.

You will want to give respect and show that you are a truly good spirit. You will see that by being good to others, you will in return get a sense of goodness and belonging in the end. You will feel better and be able to express your true inner self without hiding anything. You can bring your inner beliefs out and show others love and support at the same time.

What is your purpose in life and how to find it

We may all struggle at some point in life about what we want to do and how to do it. We may not know what our purpose is from the beginning, but with a little bit of work, we can find out what we want from life. It can be something that we want to do as a job or as a person, but getting to the purpose in life is something that we must do for our own happiness and well-being.

There is usually a purpose behind everything. We may think about doing something and we may not know if we should or not. There are things that hold us back in life and we should not let them keep up from finding our happiness and getting to all of the goals that we have dreamed about for so long. We should want to be happy and want to find out what the purpose in our life is all about.

We can conduct a survey on our life and figure out what we are doing wrong. Some people believe that they are put here for a reason and even if they are not sure what it is, they are determined to find it. They may want to take a good hard look at their life and find something that they think would be beneficial to others and to themselves as well. Getting to the purpose in life is something that is not easy, but it is well worth it when you finally figure out a reason behind the greatness that you deserve in life.

Many people think that their purpose in life is their career. They may want to do something great and achieve high honor in the job that they do everyday. They may want to save lives, teach children, preach the gospel or fight for certain causes. These are all great careers to choose and they may or may not be the right path for you to take. You may want to think about what you like to do and find a reason for doing it. You may want to think about what you can achieve in the life that you are leading now and what good can come out of it.

When you are sure that you are ready to take on the world and all the challenges in it, you should make sure that you have a goal set in life. You need to set a path for the purpose that you are on and why. You need to figure out how you can find out what you were put here to do and go after it. Once you know what you need to do, you will soon see that you have done what you need to in order to make your reason for being here on earth a great one.

You do not have to sit back and let life happen. When you want more and think that you deserve more, you should do what you think is right and move on. You should go after certain dreams and find ways to let others know that you are serious about life and the opportunities that are behind it. You need to find ways to make your purpose in life one that you can be proud of. Even if it is something small, finding your purpose will give you a feeling of accomplishment and achievement. This is something that everyone deserves to feel in his or her lifetime.

You do not have to be a super star in life, all you really have to do is go out there and be the best that you can. Have compassion and find ways to make your life better by doing what you were intended to do on this earth.

What you hold dear in life may not really be what you should hold dear

There are many things that we hold dear in our life. We may have special family members or friends that are very important to us. When we are putting these people first in our life, we are showing respect and love for them as they deserve. We need to share hopes and dreams with these people and give them the love and respect that they deserve in life. However, we do not want to be putting all our time and effort into these people because they are not the only things in life that we have to think about. We need to put focus on ourselves and what we can do to make our own life better.

Some people hold material things in life dear to them. They may have a certain passion for their cloths, car, jewelry, and many other materialistic things that have no real meaning to them. We may not be using our best judgment when all we have to think about is what we can get out of life and not what we put into it. We cannot take the material things with us when we go. We need to put them aside and move on to other more important things that we should be concentrating on.

Having love and peace in life is far more important than materials. We need to experience the feeling of being loved and giving love as well. These are thing that we need to hold dear to our hearts so that we are able to be more complete in life and to have what we need. We can make memories with our friend and family members. These memories are going to be something that we have for a long time to come.

Goals are important to hold dear as well. We need to think about our future and what we can do to better improve it. We have to be willing to put some hard work into what we want from life and go after it from there. We have to set these goals and make them a reality so that we are better able to make a better life for ourselves.

There are plenty of people that are in a relationship that is no good. These relationships are what can damage their life and make them feel bad about who they are. These are not things that they should be holding dear to themselves. It is crucial in life to make sure that you are giving as much as you are receiving so that you can feel better as a person. How you are feeling is going to make up for a lot of the way you express things to others. You want other people around you to feel good and this is something that you can feel good about.

Many times people get caught up in the crazy world around them. They may forget about what is really important and what they need to be doing. It is hard for some people to think about other things that are more important than a career or money.

We have to think about what makes us who we are. Being self-involved and forgetting about those around us that we love and care about is not the right answer. We need to find ways to make life better and to bring the things that we hold dear closer to us.

Make the time to spend with your loved ones and make happiness your number one goal in life.

How to feel more alive daily

There are many people that wake up each day with the same attitude over and over. They are not thrilled with the adventure that life has put before them. They are not sure what they are doing and they feel as if they have hit a low point in life. Some people just go about their daily routine and never think about what they could really be doing if they just put their mind to it.

It is important to feel good about life and to go about it with full force and fun. You need to think positively so that you are able to achieve the goals that you have dreamed about for such a long time. You should not sit back and just let life happen to you. You need to take charge and make your life happen. You want to be successful and at the same time, you want to have fun and enjoy the ride as you go.

You want to feel alive every day. You want to be more alive than just breathing, you want to have the power and the strength to feel great and be energetic with the life that you are leading. There are so many ways to find a reason to be happy and excited about the day that you are living. Each day that you wake up should be a great one just because you are there to share it with the rest of the world. You should be excited about being alive and living your life to the fullest with each moment.

Thinking positively is one way to have a happy and energetic day, however you will find that you need more than just that. You may need some physical help to make your life more than just another day at work or home with the kids. You will need to make your physical appearance more alive and thrilling. You should do something that gets your blood moving. You will want to find some kind of exercise so that you are able to make your body more alive and more efficient for the day ahead.

Many people turn to vitamins for help with energy and excitement. However this is not the answer for some. There is nothing wrong with taking some vitamins to help perk up your spirits, however you may need to have the right way of thinking so that you are able to keep your mind in the happy mode and moving along as you want. You want to find things that give you joy and bring you more alive. This can be anything in life that you feel has meaning to it and makes you happy.

Take in each day that you are alive and think of it as an opportunity. You will not be around forever and you want to make the most of each day that you have. If you are sharing that life with someone else, you will want to find ways to include them and make memories that will last forever. This can be with your partner, friend, child or even someone that you work with. You want to make life better for everyone and feel more alive with each breath that you take. You will see that you will have a happier and maybe even a much healthier life when you use the good in life to your advantage. You will find more success and be the person that you have always wanted to become. You will see the changes not just in you, but in the people that you touch on daily basis as well.

How to make others feel more alive by what you say in life

It is important to think about the things that we say to others in life. We want to make sure that we are not hurting other by the terrible things that we say. Sometimes, we may not even realize what we are doing at the time, however it is something that we should think about so that we are not making it hard for others to be happy.

There is no sense in life to make other people miserable. This is not something that you should want to do. You should try and make the way that you treat others a positive experience. You will get better feedback when you are nicer to others and you are giving them the respect and love that they deserve. You will want to think about what you can do to help them be happy and this in turn will reflect on you.

Showing others kindness is very crucial to being a good person. We want to make sure that we are treating others, as we would like to be treated. We need to say nice things and be positive when we are speaking to others. You have to find ways to give them energy from the comments that you make. You want to give them hope and help them feel more alive by giving them encouraging words to get them through anything.

You want to be upbeat when you are trying to help someone achieve goals in life. You will want to let them know that you are there for them and that you want to help them get exactly to where they want to be. It may mean that you will have to show some compassion and give your help to others when they need it. This is not something that is too hard. All you really have to do is find a way to say nice things and to be positive. You can make a lot of good come from the positive things that you say to another person.

Giving great talks that will show enthusiasm and life is something that you should try to do when you can. It will make no difference that you are talking to. You will want to make sure that you are giving them the help that they need when they need it. This means that you do not want to be negative just because something bad has happened. You will want to find a way to work through it and make the best of the situation.

You will defiantly need to be positive when you are talking and dealing with children. You will want to make sure that you are helping them think good thoughts so that they can get to where they want to be in life. You will see that the encouragement that you give them now will help them throughout their life. This positive energy will stay with them as they grow and make new decisions in life. You will see that you can make a lot of difference by showing someone that you are there for them and are giving them support.

Finding ways to stay upbeat is very important. You should try and avoid anyone or anything that is very stressful on your life. You will want to keep your views on life positive and always thinking that things are going to improve. When you are willing to keep these feelings and thoughts around, you will see that you can get to where you want to be in life and you will also be helping others feel good about who they are and what they want to become.

How to change your unhappy life

If you are not happy in life, you will have no one to blame but yourself. You are the one person that is responsible for the way that you are feeling in life. You control your destiny and you will want to make sure that you are living your life the way that you have dreamed about. You will not want to settle for anything less than what you want. You will want to be happy and you need to find ways to make this happen for you.

If you are living in an unhappy life, you need to start setting goals that will help you succeed. You will want to be someone that you can be proud of and that others will be proud of as well. When you are using your best potential to be happy, you will find that you are able to make your life better and get more than what you ever expected.

You should not worry about what other people think. You need to make yourself happy and forget about what others want. However, you want to be respectful so that you are not hurting others along the way. You want to succeed and have a happy life, but never at the expense of someone else. You should think about what you can do in life to make your happiness a priority without hurting anyone else.

Find things that make you smile. You should concentrate on the goals that you have that would make you a better person. You may want to find ways to be successful. This may mean that you have to further your education and get a better job. You may find that you are not happy in your career and this can be something that makes you very unhappy in life. If you want to be happier, you should think about what you really want to do and go after it. This will get you the self-respect and courage that you have been looking for.

If you are in a relationship that is not good, you should think about getting out of it. You need to be around people that bring you up and not take you down. You need to have the relationships in your life that give you joy and comfort. You will find that once you rid yourself of the bad spirits that you are associated with, you will have an easier time being happy and following through with your plans and dreams that you have set for yourself.

Get your life on track. You should think about the things that you could do for your emotional and the physical part of your life. You want to make sure that you are getting the emotional support that is vital to living a happy and healthy life. You will find this type of support from other people that want you to do well and be happy in life. These people are your friends and family that have stuck by you through thick and thin.

You will also want to keep your physical side in good shape too. You want to exercise and keep your body healthy. This is something that will give you a positive outer being. When you look good, you will feel good. You want to keep your body fit and looking just like you want it to. Your outside image will reflect on others and this will in turn give you more of a positive inner being too. You will be happier in your life and you will have a better chance at succeeding and being the person that you want to be.

How to Learn the truth about life

Life is not always as we expect. There are many myths at time about the truth of life. Sometimes we do not have things turn out the way that we would like them to however it is important to understand what life is all about. We may learn this lesson on our own or have the help of others. Sometimes people are not sure what is right and what is wrong but with a little help, they can find the right road to travel.

We all have questions about life. Sometimes we can be confused and not sure of what we should do in certain instances. It is hard to figure out what we should be doing all the time. We may need to do some looking until we find exactly what we should be doing with our life. It may take some hardships at first, but after a while, we can learn about what to do.

Some people think that life is going to hand them things. They may believe that they deserve to have certain things given to them. When we want something, it is important to know that we work hard for it so that we can achieve the goals that are most important. It may take losing something that we love to understand what life is all about. The truth about life is not always easy.

Gaining control of your life is achievable. You can learn about what is important and follow your dreams. You need to realize that life is not going to hand you all that you want and that you may have to work hard at it. You will see that you can improve your life on your own and make things happen for you that you want. You will see that you are in control and you need to make important goals and dreams come true.

You can learn a lot about life just by listening to others. You can see how other people make mistakes and how they can change things for the better. You can learn from others and take their advice to help you achieve the things in life that you want. You will see that you can learn what life is really about. Learning from others is very important. You can get things from them that you would not be able to learn about in any book or magazine.

When bad things happen in our life, we do not have to take them as tragedies. We can use this experience and make it something great. We do not have to get down and feel bad about these things. We can use these times to learn a lesson and make a bad time turn into a good one. It is important to see that you can learn about truth very quickly even if you do not want to.

There is nothing wrong with wanting more out of life. You do not have to settle for what it just gives you. You can work hard and make things happen for you. It is very necessary to take your life seriously and make things happen when you want them to. You do not have to just sit back and let life happen to you. You can take control and make the important goals that you have dreamed about work out for your life in the end.

How to discover that beauty is not everything

It is important to know that beauty on the outside is not everything. This is not the most important thing in the world. There are a lot of people that believe that they have to be beautiful on the outside so that people will notice them and like them. This is not the truth. It is important for people to understand that they do not have to be perfect in order for them to be great.

It is not always evident from the beginning that beauty on the outside is not important. This may take a little while to realize before the reality finally sets in. there is more to life than just good looks. A person has to be good on the inside in order to be the best that they can be. There are many in the world that forgets this fact and they may get a little carried away with their outer beauty.

It is a good thing to learn in life that they way you look does not have to be the deciding factor in how you live. You need to make sure that you are doing what you need to so that you are able to have a happy and fulfilling life. You need to make the most of what you have and be very grateful for it. You cannot change the way that you look in most cases, however you can change the way that you act and the personality that you have towards others.

Getting more out of life is very important. You cannot rely on the beauty that you have on the outside to get you what you want. You need to work on education, compassion, and love so that you make all of your dreams and goals happen in life. You need to make others aware of your inner being so that you are able to truly shine through and make them see how wonderful you are.

If you think that you can have success just by putting on make up and wearing all the right clothes, you are very wrong. There is so much more to a great life. You need to have the right way of thinking so that you cannot only be good to yourself, but good to others as well. You cannot go through life being mean to the world because of the way that they look. You need to realize that there is so much more to a person than just their hair and clothes. You need to see that there is a spiritual side to everyone.

The spiritual side to people may determine how they treat others. This is going to be the way that they think and feel in different situations. It is important to know that you have to be kind and considerate of others so that your outside beauty can be better than ever. Beauty is only skin deep. You need to know that you have to feel good about the way that you act towards others people and how you handle yourself is certain situations before you can actually be beautiful.

You may not learn all at once how to be a good person inside. If you have thought about your looks for many years, you may need to find a way to adjust to being a warm and gracious person on the inside. You need to think about what is truly important to you in your life and how you feel towards it. Once you do this, you can make your inner being shine through and make your outside appearance even better.

How to feel needed is a feeling of full life

We all would like to feel needed at some point in life. This is a good feeling to most and makes a person see that they are of help to someone in need. Doing well in the world is truly important. You need to be helpful so that you are able to see that you are special and that others depend on you for support. This is an awesome feeling that most people will feel great about. It can really lift your spirits and bring you closer to someone that you care about.

It may not happen right at first in life, but at some point we will have someone that needs us for something in his or her life. This is a step that you do not want to mess up on. You want to be a great method of support for someone that is leaning on you. It makes no difference what the need is; you have to take it seriously.

You may be needed for something minor or major. However, no matter what it is, you need to make it a priority. You have to make it something that you do with all your passion and heart, even if it something so small. You will see that when people understand that they can rely on you, they will feel closer to you and that is important. You will be needed and that makes you feel good too.

Being needed gives us a sense of security in life. This is something that makes us feel like we have a purpose. That is very crucial to being a strong person. When we have people that need us, we can feel better. This will lead us to feelings of being fulfilled. This is a great method of making the most of your life and being the person that you want to be.

Finding out about life and what it has to offer for you is something that you need to do on your own. The way that others think about you is sometimes not as important. At the end of the day, you need to feel like you have done a good job and that you are proud of all that you have achieved. When you are giving good advice and help to other when they need it, you will see that your self-esteem and pride go way up. This is going to make you a happier person too.

You do not always have to give advice to others. Just being there for them to talk to is sometimes enough. When you are willing to lend a hand and give them the support and the comfort that they are looking for in a friend or family member, this can be all they need to do better and to feel like they are loved and cared for. Making others feel good about life is very important. You will see that this will make you and them very happy and it is something that you can do for just about anyone.

Whether you are needed at work or at home, it is going to be something that will give you happiness. Being there for others is something that every human being needs to do. It is a duty and a great honor to help someone that is feeling down or needs a helping hand. It is going to be a way of showing them that you care and that you are there for them. In return, you may find that you can lean on them when you need support as well.

How your spirit gives you creative expressions

The way that you feel inside is going to shine through to the outside. It is important to feel good so that you are able to make others feel good as well. This is going to be something that you can feel proud of and be glad to do when you can. Having a good spirit is important so that you can let your creative expressions out and shows others how great life can be.

The way that you feel on the inside is going to give you the ability to let it shine through. You will see that you can bring out your personality and use it for good. You can make the happy feelings bring more fun to you and to others. However when you are down, you will also see that being down can also be seen and others may come down as well. It is important to use your spirits in a good way so that you can be a better person.

You can let your creative side come through too. You will see that when you use the good feelings that you have inside you will make great things. You can be very spontaneous and use this to surprise others and do great things. No matter how you are feeling, you can use it to be expressive in life. You can let others see what you are thinking simply by letting your creative being out. This is something that you can use to your advantage.

When you are a person that has a great creative side, you will be able to use it with just about anything. You can apply it to your job, to your friends and with your friends. You will be able to do so much with the creative side that you are hiding inside yourself. If you are not happy with the spirit that you have inside you, you can change the way that you feel and this will make a huge difference. You may need to find some help with changing the spirits inside you. This may take some time to do.

Changing your spirit is not something that you can do over night. You have to totally change the way that you think and how you react to things. You need to make your outlook on life turn around and be totally different. This is the only way that you can make your creative expressions come out and make more of the feelings that you have inside.

When you are feeling down you will see that you can do something to change this. You do not have to just bad all the time. You can make a difference by have a more creative side and putting your feelings to good use. You will be able to make others feel great too when you are using your creative side in the right way. You can bring joy to others and make them feel good about who they are when you are using all the spirits that you have for good reason.

You will be able to achieve great things if you only put your mind to it. You can do more with your life and set great goals for yourself. You will indeed be able to be more creative and use your spirits to bring happiness to you and to anyone that is around you. You will see that you will have a better life and make things great for others as well. Remember to think positive and this will give you a great inner spirit that will never go away.

How to harness your spirit

Your spirit is who you are. It is very important to let your true spirit come through so that you are being true to yourself. You will need to make sure that you are putting your spirit to good use so that you can feel good about who you are and what you are doing. Having spirit is the most important thing in your life to have. It is what defines you and makes you who you are.

Spirit can be anything from risk taking to being conservative. No matter what your true inner spirit is, you can let it shine through and feel good about who you are at the same time. You do not have to worry about how see you if you are sure that you have the spirit that makes you happy and feeling great.

Sometimes you may need to think about your spirit. Is it the right one for you? Do you think that you need to change it or harness it? If you do, you may want to try and make some changes to your life so that you are able to make the most of how you feel and what you do in life. It is important to find a way of life that makes you happy and that makes you feel proud. You need to see your vision of life and what you have planned for yourself.

You have to have the right state of mind when you are trying to lift your spirits. You need to make yourself feel good about who you are and what you are doing. This will give you what you need to make the most of your spirits. You should think about a few things first before you let your inner spirits go. You will want to ask yourself a few questions.

Are you afraid of something in your life? Are there things that you have to think about? If you are having feelings of doubt and fear, you may need to find a way to harness your spirits. You will want to think about the choices that you have made in your life and find out what you can do to make them what you want. You want to reflect on your feelings and make them clear to you and to anyone around you.

Sometimes in life, you have to take risks. If your spirit inside you is not allowing you to do this, you may want to make some changes in your life. This is very important. You will want to put all your feelings to good use for you at all times of your life. It makes no difference if you are feeling bad or feeling good. You need to use your spirits in a positive way. This will give you a feeling of satisfaction and make you feel good about who you are and what your purpose is in life.

You want to have a happy and healthy spirit. You need to make the most of your life and put your happiness first. You will see that when you are willing to make the most of your intentions, you will be able to sit back and feel good about who you are. You will have others looking up to you as well. This is a feeling that you will hold on to for the rest of your life and you will want to remember it forever.

You should also make sure that you are thinking about others and putting their feelings into consideration. If you think that you need to harness your spirits in order to spare someone else's feelings, you may need to do this. You will see that you can do well with the things that you do for yourself as well as others in life.

9 781801 549950